HOW TO SPEAK AMERICAN

By Pasquale Marcello

CONTENTS

Introduction: The Under Language

The way we speak to each other, and the ease with which we understand each other's speech is part of what defines us, as a people and as a nation. In America we speak English. However so does a large part of the world thanks to the former global empire of the British.

It has been said that the Americans and the British are two nations separated by the same language. The Irish, the Scotch, the Welsh, the New

Zealanders, the Australians, the Canadians, the sub-continental Indians, the Burmese, the Malays , the Singaporean, the South Africans, the East Africans, the Jamaicans, the British Guianese, the Pakistani, and the rest of the general world population that uses English as a business and diplomatic language all speak English.

The fact is they just don't speak English like Americans do; nor do they understand us when we speak to them. (Except maybe for the Canadians who are almost like us but more uptight... I mean reserved.) We all know this to be so.

What makes us so different is the fact that we Americans possess all these old sayings, aphorisms, idiomatic expressions, acronyms, common sense turn-of-phrase, and slang. Even the word "slang" is a made-up term which describes how we bend and fracture the language in our everyday speech and interpersonal conversations.

These terms and phrases are literally built into our everyday lives. They come from all over the melting pot. They come from the mother countries, from business and science, and industry and technology, and the media and the arts. But mostly they come from us, originating in America, and they are constantly evolving and expanding as our common American experience flows along time. But mostly they come from everyday people just *hanging out together.* There it happened again. It's almost impossible to escape these "American-isms." They're woven into the very fabric of our everyday life. I call it the "Under Language."

The Under Language is the linguistic underpinnings of the American experience. It includes all aspects of our culture... love, sex, war, technology, social interactions, politics, and yes, by all means money, and of course most importantly our need to succeed. It describes our human abilities sacrifice, courage, loyalty, character, integrity, or lack thereof.

Taken together all these terms form a vast fabric of linguistic infrastructure whereby each word or phrase is like a gateway into the human mind. Each term invokes mental images of human situations or conditions which we all as Americans immediately recognize and identify. This tends to bind us together and make communication easier between people of all walks of life, even extremely divergent individual types.

A concept that might require a broad cross-section of knowledge or vocabulary can be easily communicated in a single word or phrase. The widespread use of these particular groups of words is an integral part of what makes us Americans different from all the other English-speaking peoples. We Americans even have a slang term for all these words phrases and clichés and expressions. We call it straight talk.

Straight talk is one of the built-in checks and balances

against spin, and sophistry, and Orwellian Newspeak, and all other forms of doubletalk, which we call bullshit. Americans do not like obfuscation.

If you want to be understood by Americans then you must talk straight, and you will hit the mark every time. If you know how to speak American, it is always possible to emphasize or make your point in a less than erudite way and yet reach everyone. The only downside to the use of these terms and phrases is that many of them involve crude or demeaning obscenities and profanity.

The thing is that if you talk to Americans this way using the clichés, they will hear you, and they will understand.

The important thing about expressing yourself in the vernacular is to know when to deliver the punch line. The correct word or phrase delivered at the most pregnant moment for maximum effect achieves desired results almost every time.

Most of the time it is comedic or satirical in nature but very often it is derisive in tone. In a society obsessed with political correctness, politically incorrect or even

downright vulgar remarks
always carry certain risks.

But so what? What the hell?

Sometimes people just need
to hear it, if only to shake
them up. The point is, you
don't have to have a Harvard
degree or 300-year-old
blueblood pedigree or
achieve superstardom in
sports or pop culture to be
hip. You just have to be one of
us and that means knowing
the things we know.

On Being American

Americans are created in four basic ways. One, you start out as a *bun in the oven* after your dad *knocked up* your mom, probably in the back of a pickup truck at a drive-in movie or after the Super Bowl.

Two, you marry an American overseas and *get brung* here.

Three, you're a *greenhorn* off the boat.

Four you crossed illegally from Mexico or Canada and

successfully acquired a *fake ID* and shortly afterwards a nice federal, state or union job.

Once here—born, brung, or snuck in—you begin your journey to cultural, economic and social assimilation. It helps to be bright, or rather quick on the uptake. Because there is an awful lot you need to know if you are ever going to *make it.*

First, you have to *get it.* Or *get with it.* Or *get hip* to what's going down and going on around you. In order to get it, you have to talk like us. You have to "speak American," otherwise you are just

another foreigner, or
Egghead, or Effete Snob, or
Ivy League aristocrat, or
worst of all—a *Square*.

Once you are actually here in
America the possibilities are
endless. In the "Land of the
Free and the Home of the
Brave" it is truly possible to
be anyone or anything you
want to be. We call it the
"American Dream." But first
you have to learn how. This
means a few basic rules have
to be observed and certain
common reference points
must be recognized.

It all starts with *attitude*.
Attitude is vital, it helps one
navigate the treacherous

currents of life's uncertainties and many adversities .In America, we have winners and losers. Attitude determines which one you will ultimately become.

"Winners never quit and losers never win." Success makes you a winner, *screwing up* makes you a loser. Winners never pass up a *good thing*. Losers never *pick up* on what they are doing wrong. They just don't get it.

Politics

In the Old West, there were certain characters, who traveled around selling so-called "magic elixirs." They promised that for a dollar, two bits, six bits, or whatever amount, the stuff was guaranteed to solve all your problems and ailments. Those men were called "Snake Oil Salesman."

Today we call them politicians.

This includes all of our public officials, from the President and Vice-President to the Cabinet to the many appointed functionaries, the Congress, and all their hired staff. Then you have the judicial system, including the judges and all the hired clerks and attorneys. There are also the state governments, governors and state legislators and more judges, more attorneys, mayors, police commissioners, city and county councilman, right down to the lowliest magistrate.

They are all snake oil salesman.

Some of them are even what we call "nice guys." But most of them are what we call "smooth sons of bitches." They will say anything to get elected or appointed. They are very big on making promises. Once in office, however, they tend to concentrate their efforts on fund raising and public image and wax ever increasingly more adept at political correctness and spin. They are all very good at spending other peoples' (the tax payers') money.

At this point in American history, the crap has gotten so deep that the average American could describe his attitude towards his leaders in three short words—cynicism, apathy, and disgust with corruption and incompetence thrown in, to give it body.

It was not always like this.

When it comes to politics, the American people represent the most diverse collection of political opinions and attitudes on earth. We have an old saying, "Opinions are like ass holes everybody's got one." We've got 300 million Americans, so we have 300 million opinions, or ass holes take your pick.

We've got them all—Democrats, Republicans, Independents, radicals, extremists, nationalists, racists, both white (the supremacists) and black militants. We've got militant feminists, militant gays, anarchists, and a very large group we call undecided. It's a miracle that the damn thing works at all—that we owe to the founding fathers.

The founding fathers numbered among the best informed and educated men of their time. Being well-versed in Latin, the founding fathers chose to model their new nation on the Roman Republic.

It was a good start.

The document they created, the United States Constitution has managed to weather over two centuries of the most turbulent times human civilization has ever known. As the Roman Republic was weaned on war, so was the American Republic. As the Roman Republic grew to be the mightiest power of its time. Ditto for the American Republic. As the Roman Republic grew and evolved its social and political institutions, it suffered the stress of expansion. The same has held true for the American Republic.

History tells us that the Roman Republic failed at the peak of its power but not of its wealth. It is known that burgeoning wealth contributed to the moral decline of the Romans and thereafter the disintegration of their empire. It is to be hoped that the American Republic has not yet reached either the peak of its power or of its wealth.

It is also known that incompatible factionalism drove the Romans to Civil War and ultimately tyranny. America has now reached a stage in her history where political factionalism threatens the basic stability of the nation.

American history has witnessed the struggle of political factions influencing the direction and evolution of our society. From the very beginning, it was a two-party system. On the one hand, you had the Whigs, and on the other the Federalists. The Whigs believed that the less government you had the better off you are. This is known in the history books as Laissez-Faire.

The Federalists favored a strong central government with a strong central bank. This battle was fought over the first 50 years of our history. Up to the Civil War, it was more or less a draw. The two parties morphed into the Republicans and Democrats, and the victory of the union established the federal government as the dominant power in American politics from then on.

The irony of it all was that the Republicans (formerly Whigs) ended up protecting and establishing federalism. The Democrats (former Federalists) ended up as the party of the working man and individual and states' rights.

Now, in the 21st century, it looks like the parties have morphed again with the Democrats espousing principles of so-called "Progressivism" which is more like European Marxist collectivism than American frontier democracy.

The Republican Party once known for its right-wing "good-ol'-boys" club is morphing into a party of the working middle class and the overburdened American taxpayer.

In order to enter politics, ancient Romans had a system known as the Cursus Honorum or "the path of honor." The Romans made no distinction between civilian or military rank. The idea was to serve the state and thereby gain reputation, wealth, and ultimately power.

Americans do it essentially the same way, except military rank is considered a separate career path. The way Americans do it makes us more colorful.

In the beginning, Americans were called upon to serve at the behest of their peers. Over time it has evolved into a path of social and economic advancement. It's called "stumping."

Stumping begins when you "throw your hat into the ring" and lets people know you're ready to work for them. You go around shaking hands, kissing babies, and making speeches. You tell them what they want to hear and "the sky is the limit." If you come out of nowhere you are "a dark horse." If you're rich and popular and your family is influential they call you "a favorite son." If you win it all, they call you "the People's choice." Every American politician worth his salt knows that "you can fool some of the people some of the time, but you can't fool all of the people all the time." But they still try!

In America, we don't have any such thing as the cursus honorum. This is well reflected by the fact that Americans generally do not consider politics to be an honorable career. Oh yeah, we let them throw out the first baseball and we do news pieces when they go jogging or play basketball.

We know they always show up and take a bow at important public events like new blockbuster movies or championship sporting events, launching space missions, or new building commemorations, or when breaking bottles of champagne over the bows of new ships. Every night, we listen to the political news with a "tin ear" and "take what they say with a grain of salt." But the truth is, "we are just not that into them."

This is because life in America is not about politics, and it never really has been. America is about individuality, seeking fortune, pursuing happiness, about creating and living the dream. As a vocation, politics ranks right up there on the stink meter with people like lawyers, tax collectors, bill collectors, door-to-door salesman, and other various types of con men. Basically we view politicians and government itself as a necessary but unpleasant intrusion into our personal lives.

Americans just don't like politicians.

They tend to spend a lot of time "double-talking" and "double-dealing." They pay a lot of lip service to disadvantaged minorities because we all know "the squeaky wheel gets the grease."

We also know that politicians like to be "greased" too. When politicians and their "cronies" (cronies being all the people that hang around politicians to help get them elected) "jump on the bandwagon," and become entrenched in their offices, we call it "feeding at the public trough." When they take the financial "kickbacks" and special contributions (payola) we call it "graft."

As things go along in the government's endless search for increased revenues, the cronies think up new ways to slip their hands into our pockets. The politicians tout these ways as "the greatest thing since sliced bread." When they screw up and the taxpayer has to pick up the bill, they have their cronies in the press "put a positive spin" on the story so they come out "smelling like a rose." We are supposed to love them for it.

We don't.

Remember what we said in the beginning. Americans like straight talk, not double talk, not double dealing, we prefer communication without obfuscation.

In short, government and the politicians that operate that way represent Big Brother. With the technology available today, Big Brother is way, way, way "too much with us."
So "the beat goes on." They tell us this. They tell us that. They promised us this. They promise us that. But, "the more things change, the more they stay the same."

"Bottom line" is the whole damn system is "FUBAR."

Take health care for instance, it's not really about health, it's not really about care, it's really about profits and divvying up the pie. New rules such as "no more pre-existing conditions," sound cool... a guy can be a drug addict for 35 years, no problem! The taxpayers get the old "put the load on me."

 Oh yeah everybody has to pay whether they want to or not. Question: "What is wrong with this picture? "Answer: "Nothing is wrong; this is the New World order. This is what we call 'change.'"

Sounds more like somebody "is dealing from the bottom of the deck."

Not to worry, getting it wrong is an American political tradition. After all, the only way you learn is by your mistakes. If it feels good do it. If it looks right, it is right. After all, nobody is perfect. We are all human. People make mistakes and politicians are just people. Just the same we only trust them as far as we can throw them. In God we trust, it says so right on our money. We aren't kidding around when we talk about the "almighty buck."

Cops and Feds Versus Criminals and Gangsters

We love our gangsters. We love their toughness. We admire their attitude—grit in their personality that only comes from the street. We admire their defiance of the system. We laugh at their comic characterizations. We abhor their brutality and violence. Nevertheless we tend to view them as the underdog and sometimes we can't help but root for them.

In a way, we admire their ruthlessness, but only because of their efficiency in achieving their purpose and solving their problems.

Psychotic criminals are another story. These people intrigue us, and frighten us, and also tend to frustrate our sense of right and wrong by the coddling they receive from the legal system. Psychopathic serial killers have always held a special fascination. From Lizzie Borden, to Richard Speck,   Jeffrey Dahmer, Charles Manson, the Boston strangler, the Hillside stranglers,   the night stalker, and the Green River killer, we see a literal personification of evil in the form of the insane irrational mind turned loose.

We tend to view these people in simplistic terms. We say, "That one wasn't playing with a full deck," or "He had a screw loose," or "Here's another whack job," or "Another escapee from the loony bin," or simply, "He's nuts, crazy, gone, a freak, a serious head case, a loony tune, or a cuckoo." They make great material for books and movies and TV shows.

It's different with gangsters (the old-time gangsters, not the modern drug czars.) We tend to romanticize them. We tend to overlook their flaws because secretly, we admire and envy both their methods and their results. This form of hero worship goes back to our frontier and immigrant culture where disadvantaged but rugged individuals were able to somehow overcome adversity in spite of the deck being stacked against them.

They are not afraid of the law, nor do they shrink from violence in order to impose their will and get their way. Gangsters carry guns. They pack heat; they use the artillery whenever necessary. They don't play games with their enemies. They get the job done, and they care little for who doesn't like it.

It's no cakewalk. "The Man" is formidable.
The cops and the Feds have electronic
eyes and ears everywhere, plus
undercover agents and snitches who wear
wires. Gangsters rarely survive long, and
they rarely live to old age, unless it's in
prison.

The unwritten law is, "If you squeal, if you
sing, if you make like a stool pigeon, if you
cop a plea and turn state's evidence, your
life is not worth a plug nickel." Once they
find out you broke the code, they "put a
contract out on you." Now you are fair
game. There are "button men" on the
street looking for you 24/7. The police
cannot protect you. If you're lucky, they
put you in the witness protection
program and they bury you in some out-
of-the-way corner in some out-of-the-way
hick town.

We know that women are romantically
attracted to gangsters. They get the "hots"

for the forbidden fruit. We like gangster
chicks, the gun malls, hoofers, and
strippers because they are always good
looking and tend to wear cute clothes, no
clothes, or spandex and they definitely
positively "put out."

On top of this, these women tend to see
and appreciate the tortured soul—the
nice little boy persona—in even the
meanest, nastiest bad guy. They forgive
them their transgressions and pray for
their souls—at least until they catch them
cheating or "two-timing." Then look out,
it's Katie bar the door, and hell hath no
fury. *Fuggedaboudit.*

Bottom line is we are intrigued with them
subliminally and consciously. Because
let's face it.

They have the guts and nerve to disobey.

Guns, Missiles, Rockets, and Other Phallic Obsessions

From school-prank spit balls and pea shooters to Iowa class 16-inch rifles Americans love firepower.

We love symbols of firepower too. Consider "the Empire State building" and other skyscrapers. What are these things but symbols of potency? We like big cars, big ships, big airplanes, big houses, big ranches, big freeways, big tits (the only un-phallic exception), big names, big bank accounts, and of course big dicks.

But it's the firepower—the guns, the missiles, the rockets, and the bombs that fascinate and when necessary, prevail.

Just cruise along the list of American weapons.

You got your Kentucky rifles, your Colt peacemakers, your Winchester repeaters, your Browning automatics, your Thompson submachine guns (sometimes known as the Chicago typewriter), your .38 caliber snub nose, your M-1's, your M-16's, and best of all, your .44 magnum—the gun that can "blow your head clean off."

You got your army guns, your Navy guns, your Air Force missiles, your sub-launched missiles, your air-launched missiles, your MIRVs, ICBMs and last, but most important, antimissile missiles.

Our ultimate phallic demonstration was the Saturn five. The Apollo moon missions were the ultimate demonstration of American potency. We added in a special touch by driving our "moon buggies" all over the lunar dust.

Look out world, the Americans are coming! "Lafayette we are here," "I shall return," "One small step." We come on horseback with pistols and rifles. We come in DUK's with battleship back-up. We come in aircraft carriers. We come in stealth bombers and fighters. That's when you never see us coming. Then it's over.

After the bad guys have been introduced to the infernal regions we say, "Give me a vector; I'm coming home." It's "Miller time!"

WHAT IS A GOOD DEAL?

What is a good deal?

Everybody wants one.

In selling school they teach you that a good deal is "whatever the customer thinks is a good deal."

Diplomats will tell you that a good deal is whenever two sides come to an agreement whereby each side thinks they have secured some type of advantage in the outcome.

Real estate people would say a good deal is when a purchaser secures a below market price, or a seller achieves an above market compensation.

Police hostage negotiators will tell you a good deal is any deal that preserves life or prevents injury or property damage.

Criminal Defense attorneys would say any deal which keeps their clients out of jail or reduces jail sentences is a good deal. Criminal prosecutors like deals which favor the state's public image and improve political approval ratings.

In America, there are all kinds of deals. There are good deals, bad deals, raw deals, fair deals, shady deals, and profitable deals.

Obviously, a deal is some kind of agreement made between various parties on a variety of subjects. As Americans, we are always on the lookout for good deals. Conversely we are always trying to be cognizant of and thereby avoid bad deals.

Whenever there is a disagreement which
we wish to settle amicably we say, "Let's
make a deal." FDR gave us the "New Deal."

Al Capone and Lucky Luciano thought
they got "raw deals."

When we buy our cars and houses we
shop for "the best deal."

Retailers advertise unbelievably great
deals. (If it sounds too good to be true it
usually is.)

Professional athletes, TV and film
celebrities, and corporate executives sign
lucrative deals.

Unions threatened to go on strike in order
to secure good deals for their members.

But let the buyer beware. There are always those underhanded skunks who try to "deal from the bottom of the deck."

The whole thing about dealing is getting the other side to think that they are receiving the better part of the bargain. Hence the term "confidence man."

We have different kinds of dealers. We have equipment dealers. We have car dealers. We have diamond dealers. We have drug dealers. And we have unethical dealers of all sorts.

When you deal, you are making a pitch. You lay it out for the other side. You try to make it look too good to pass up. Some dealers adhere strictly to the twin edicts "there's a sucker born every minute "and its corollary "never give a sucker an even break."

When you go on a successful run we say you're "wheeling and dealing." When they offer us something we want we say "now you're talking" or "That's what I'm talking about."

When you come to the end, before you make your decision or afterwards when it's too late, we say, "It is what it is." And if you want to put your two cents in as a third-party adviser you say, "I'm just saying."

When friends come up to us to tell us about their success, we say, "Good deal!" like it's a blessing. And of course every good deal comes with one extra "to boot" that amounts to "the icing on the cake."

Sometimes the news is not good and we hear about somebody "losing his or her ass" in a bad deal.

When we need explanations we ask,
"What's the deal?"

American history is chock full of deals.

Ulysses S. Grant's deal was "unconditional surrender."

Teddy Roosevelt made a great deal with Panama.

The invention of limited term financing for homes and automobiles was a great deal for the American standard of living.

Henry Ford's invention of mass production lines in order to lower prices on the Model T.'s was a great deal for the American consumer.

Gen. George Marshall made Western Europe and Japan "a deal they couldn't refuse."

Lyndon Johnson's great Society was a great deal for long- disadvantaged population segments.

The American Indians got a raw deal all along the line. So did the African-Americans until the civil rights movement changed things.

The deal that has kept us all alive since 1945 is known as MAD mutually assured destruction. It is not so much a deal as a threat.

Surely the greatest deal of all time was the one offered by Jesus said, "Believe in me and you will live forever." That's not a deal, either, but it was one hell of a promise.

It's up to us to close the deal. Or as we say in America, "Done deal."

CAR WARS

Americans love their cars. Americans are car crazy. Automobiles are held in the highest esteem, right up there with mom's cooking, the family pets, baseball, football, straight A's, and Old Glory.

The automobile came to America along with the 20th century via the Industrial Revolution. Humanity's greatest leap forward, after fire, was the invention of the wheel. In the beginning, wheels needed hoof and manpower. Then came steam, first ships, and then railroads. Then came electricity, and we had electric trains and trolleys to move us about. Then came the internal combustion engine.

The automobile revolutionized personal transportation by dislodging its predecessor the horse. We may have used horses to conquer the continent, but the horseless carriage conquered us.

It was now possible for any individual to travel anywhere he or she wished to go, at any time of day or night, in any season and in any weather. All you needed was a road leading you there and enough fuel to get to there. The car changed the entire culture beginning with the economy.

First of all, enough cars for everybody meant mass production. Mass production meant lower prices. Lower prices meant increased demand for more production and growth. Growth meant more jobs.

Of course more roads were needed. Raw materials were needed to sustain production. All kinds of new things needed to be invented and produced. We invented gas stations; we built roadside restaurants and motels. We invented drive-ins, car radios, car air-conditioning, highway signs, and stoplights.

We became a mobile society. We created the first really large labor force of technically and mechanically trained men. This was to stand us in good stead when fighting the industrial wars of the 20th century. All through the 20th century the manufacture of trucks and cars powered the economy.

The interstate system connected it all together. Suburban and industrial sprawl lights up the North American continent at night so much that it can be seen from space.

Car culture just keeps us inventing new things like family vacations at theme parks like Disneyland. Beach resorts and ski lodges suddenly became closer and easier to get to. Ditto for the National Parks.

Americans like to drive fast. Gangsters and getaway cars drove fast. Rum runners during Prohibition drove fast. Moonshiners trying to escape the cops drove fast. Teenagers in the 40s and 50s and 60s and 70s and 80s and on up to now like to drag race—they drive fast. Impatient commuters on the Interstate try to drive fast. Heroes in the movies always drive fast and stuntmen stage horrific wrecks.

But The Man, Smokey the Bear, and State Troopers everywhere, and small-town cops don't like people to drive fast. Clever Orwellian government officials are busy installing ticket cameras at as many intersections as possible. Insurance companies monitor citations always prepared to increase rates on transgressors.

Driving under the influence fast leads to jail. God help you if you hurt somebody. You deserve whatever you get. Speeding fines, accident risk, jail time, it doesn't matter—we still like to drive fast. But God help you if you pass a school bus.

Americans love racing. Indy cars, Pro Stock, fueled dragsters, even big diesels. We love to watch them put the pedal to the metal and go roundy-round. Speed is empowerment, whether you're behind the wheel yourself or watch them go by at 200+ m. p. h. engines screaming in your ears and the smell of fuel exhaust offending your nostrils. Speed is empowerment. Americans are all about power.

Cars do a lot for us and it goes way beyond simple transportation and personal convenience. You can tell a lot about people from the kind of car they drive. In LA they say you are what you drive. That makes sense coming from an image-conscious city built around freeways and based on dreams, fantasies, and mass-market promotions.

"Looked at my watch and it was quarter to five rollin' like a mustang on a four day drive," Chuck Berry, *Reelin' and Rockin'* lyric.

"The motor cooled down, the heat went down, and that's when I heard that highway sound. The Cadillac a-sittin' like a ton of lead, a hundred and ten a half a mile ahead. The Cadillac lookin' like it's sittin' still, and I caught Maybelline at the top of the hill," Chuck Berry, *Maybellene* lyric.

We are a car culture. We love our cars. We make songs about them. We do everything in cars. Yes everything. We go parking, to drive-ins, more parking, vacations, shopping (lots of shopping), parking, making out, getting to first base, going all the way. Whoops now she's knocked up and her dad is going to shoot you if you don't do the right thing.

If you really want insight into the symbiotic relationship between Americans and their cars you should speak to the people who sell them to us. The American car salesman is an entrenched part of the American landscape and also the American vernacular. Let's hear from one of them now.

CAR WARS   by Fast Willie, the Car Salesman

Elvis loved Cadillacs and so do I. In fact I was once known as "The Guru of Cadu." I've got two of them now, a new one and an old one.

The new one is a black 2011 CTS which stands for "Cadillac Touring Sedan." The old one is a 1988 Carmine-red Coupe DeVille with white leather guts, wire wheels, real chrome bumpers, and a silky smooth 4.5 L aluminum V-8. I like them both, but neither one of them really fits the definition of a Cadillac.

The CTS is an ersatz BMW, alias European sport-sedan trendy car. The Coupe DeVille is like a Treaty battleship, cut down by Washington government. But there was a time... Oh yes, there was a time when a *Cadillac* was the reigning queen of the auto fleets of the world.

Cadillac is named after the Marquis de Cadillac, who founded "la cite de la trois rivieres," Detroit for short. In the beginning, there was the big three— General Motors, Ford, and Chrysler. Between them were offered enough models so that whatever you drove was a clear clue to your socioeconomic status as a citizen.

In 1973 Americans bought over 13 million cars and light trucks. To give you a clue the People's Republic of China only just managed to sell 13 million like cars and trucks in 2009 after more than 30 years of breakneck economic expansion.

Back in 1973, General Motors claimed a 66% of the North American automobile market. What was good for General Motors was truly good for the USA.

That was my rookie year; that was the year I was hired to sell Oldsmobiles. Oldsmobile was known for its rocket V-8's. Buick was known for its solid, stodgy, imposing automobiles, generally purchased by doctors and senior citizens. Chevrolet was like Sears. You could buy anything from them, from the smallest

cars to the largest trucks. Pontiac made
performance machines—GTOs , Firebirds,
and Trans Ams. Cadillac was the
heavyweight. If you could afford a Caddy,
you "had arrived."

In the dictionary, Cadillac is defined as a
large, heavy American automobile. In the
world of automobile legend, Cadillac was
a tycoon's car, a gangster's car, a cross-
country touring sedan, and the chosen
livery of limo and hearse manufacturers.

You can talk about your Bentleys, and
your Daimlers, and your Maybachs of
today's elitist standards. But none of them
could make a pimple on 1976 Fleetwood
Talisman, or Fleetwood 75.

The two decades between 1955 and 1975
represent the high tide of the American
automobile industry, at least in my mind.
That was when we perfected most of our

low-maintenance, high-endurance interstate driving technology. The cars were big. It was a time of American generosity. You got a big bang for your buck.

The cars were long, low, and wide. They were powered by high- displacement overhead valve V-8's. They generally sported automatic transmissions. After 1965 air conditioning became so common that it was almost standard equipment.

In addition to all the big highway cruisers and family station wagons, these were the years when we produced the "muscle cars." First came the Thunderbirds and Corvettes. Then came the Mustang followed by the Camaro. Pontiac made the GTOs , Firebirds, Trans Ams and Grand Prix. Ford supped up the Falcons, which morphed into Torinos and Grand Torinos. Chrysler got into the act, too, with Chargers, Roadrunners, and Super Bees.

These were the cars the Baby Boomers grew up with.

Let the good times roll.

Summer could the last forever. But it was not to be. The Arabs and the oil companies were seriously jacking up the price of gasoline. The Baby Boomers were growing up and they needed small, cheap, fuel-efficient college commuter cars.

On both sides of the Atlantic, there were hungry automobile- manufacturing nations, eagerly coveting a piece of that fat, juicy, North American automobile market. We were a giant bull's-eye on their boardroom maps. The conquest of the North American automobile market and the fall of Detroit got underway in earnest in the 70s.

I was young. I had just gotten into it. I was
"fresh as a daisy, full of piss and vinegar,
"and full of fight. Little did I know I was
about to enter three and a half decades of
Sisyphusian nightmare on my way to
becoming The Existential Car Salesman.

Some people say "life is just a bowl of
cherries". Some people say "life is like a
box of chocolates." But I say, "Nothing
happens till somebody sells something."
That was the first truth I learned at
General Motors. The second truth I
learned is that when I performed the sale
of an automobile, I was closing a vast
economic loop which began with mining,
which led through the metals industry—
steel, aluminum, and copper; inclusive of
the national rail and trucking
transportation system; on to include the
electronics industry, battery technology,
computer technology, all kinds of
engineering, design, legal services,
advertising and promotions, paints and
chemicals, rubber for tires and hoses,

plastics and upholstery technology, many types of safety technology, and multiple, multiple, job titles and categories. In other words, whenever I sold an automobile or truck manufactured in this country, everybody got to work. The big executives worked; the lawyers worked; the secretaries, production people, efficiency experts, copywriters, truck drivers, railroad engineers, miners, steel workers, road and construction related industries, mechanics, managers, lots of bankers and financial people, multimedia advertising on a huge scale, and of course sales men all worked. Nothing happens till somebody sells something, that's for sure. That's for *damn* sure.

These are truths that many Americans today have forgotten or are just unaware of. What difference does that make, you say? Well I say that it is going to make a great deal of difference to a great many people. At least, that's what I said back in the day when I was a "young gun" and the car wars had just begun.

One thing every new car or truck comes with is what the customers call "that new car smell." The new car smell literally "puts you under the ether." "Puts them to sleep," we say. The new car smell hooks them, slows down their thinking, and dulls their senses, economically speaking. Makes a fool easier to separate from his money.

Each manufacturer smells different from the next and the domestics differ greatly from the foreign. The Europeans differ considerably from the Asians makes. Over the years it got to the point where if I closed my eyes, I could tell what make of car I was sitting in simply by scent.

When the first foreign cars invaded, Detroit was *not* prepared. Europe struck first with a swarm of Volkswagen Beetles and Mini-buses. They represented a cheap, no-frills transportation solution, but we fell in love with them because they were reliable and cheap. I remember when the highways were full of the sound of their four-cylinder pancake engines going gada, gada, gada, gada like a bunch of washing machines.

We fought back with Ford Falcons, Plymouth Valiants, Chevy Novas, and Chevy Corvairs. But the Corvairs were bashed really bad by Ralph Nader.

Honda showed up in the 60s with a line of 50 cc motorbikes and a three-cylinder "city car." The motorbikes got bigger and so did the cars, so that by the 70s, Honda was selling the famous Civics and Accords.

Toyota came in with a line of minimalist cars and trucks that included simple Corollas, milquetoast, plain-Jane Camrys and small, SR5 pickups. Datsun came in selling B-210s, and small pickup trucks before they changed the company name to "Nissan."

Subaru became a cult car. Ditto for Suzuki. The Koreans arrive in the late 80s with Hyundai and Kia. What started as a trickle turned into a flood that saturated the North American car market?

Adding insult to injury, the US government passed a series of laws imposing mileage restrictions on American manufacturers, while at the same time inviting foreigners to establish taxpayer-subsidized, nonunion manufacturing plants right here in the States, thereby undermining the Detroit's natural hometown advantage. On top of that, foreign companies were the

beneficiaries of all kinds of slanted ink—
paid-for propaganda, the way I saw it.

So there you are. That was the car wars, a
muddy, bloody, slugfest fought day by
day, and ditch by ditch, year in, year out,
decade after decade, and it's still going on.
Trouble is we—me and the American
guys—are losing. There are many reasons
why they "got the drop on us." It's kind of
like the Ultimate Perfect Storm. It seemed
to me as if everybody was out to get
Detroit—everybody who ever held a
grudge.

The government was against us, the oil
companies were certainly never our
friends, and the media pundits (who took
kickbacks from the foreign car companies
to propagandize their so-called bull shit
superiority) were all against us.

Then there were the college professors, smoking pipes and condemning all things American, influencing their students (my generation) to rebel and reject their parents' principles.

Then came the Yuppies who always thought they knew better than anybody else anyway, who set a new standard in perverse logic. Not cool to buy American; very cool to buy foreign. I used to marvel at the air of superiority foreign car buyers took on when they would visit our showroom. Sometimes it seemed they only showed up for the purposes of insulting us, like they got some kind of charge from putting down America. I used to think to myself who are these people?

My gut reaction was that these were ignorant, arrogant, smug, effete snobs sent to torture me by the same devils who helped the bad guys everywhere. My intellect told me that these were poor misguided souls who needed an education in the truth and set forth on the proper path to transportation redemption. In other words, they were looking for a salesman. I did my best to educate them with the facts and the truth. It didn't always work but I made sure they got an earful before they left.

I realize that saying these things might make me sound bitter. This is not the case. For 35 years I was an, insider, privy to information which neither the American consumer nor the manipulative pundits have access to. I merely tell it like it is.

I fully understand that in many cases the people from Detroit were their own worst enemies. Although I sold mostly General Motors products I've never worked directly for General Motors. I worked in the dealer system.

I like to compare the American car dealer system to the landed gentry of 19th century society. Here you have a bunch of guys running franchises. After World War II, anybody lucky enough to acquire and operate a big-three automobile franchise was virtually guaranteed big-time success. In most cases, demographics alone was enough given the postwar expansion of the American economy. So an entire new generation of millionaires was born. I think that in my brief 35 years, I worked for most of them.

Most people think that the invasion of the American market by foreign car companies hurt domestic car dealers. This is a misunderstanding; people are getting the wrong story. The simple fact is most American domestic dealers also possess foreign car franchises. Because of this, when Detroit took the hit, it hurt

American manufacturers much more than the American dealers.

The big three dealers did not fear the arrival of the imports because they already owned the franchises. The foreign automobile companies needed experienced dealers and a ready-made dealer network in order to succeed and naturally they distributed their franchises to already well-experienced American ownership. The only people who really got hurt by this were the people working in the domestic franchises, people like me, who had to stand our ground and wave the flag and take the hits, the insults, and the diminishing financial returns.

In addition, the advent of the computer changed the in-house dealership landscape by putting the bean counters and clerks in control. The focus on clout within the dealership changed from the salesman to the business manager. This meant changes in financial compensation and not for the good.

Pay scales increasingly took the shape of an inverted pyramid where the higher up you were placed, the less you did, and the more you got paid.

Remember what I said back in the beginning about the first truth? Nothing happens until somebody sells something. The salesman creates the sale, the salesman impacts the profit, the salesman puts everybody to work and justifies everybody else's job but the business manager gets the most money. What is wrong with this picture?

Office politics is a snake pit. It's a normal condition in the American office environment. So there I was -- the skeptics in front of me, scoundrels behind me. Not just me, but every American car salesman is in the same boat. There you are in the front line, out on the perimeter, shagging fly balls, manning your foxhole.

The rules are very simple. The job is commission only. No salary. So first, you have to cover the draw. You have to meet your quota and hit the bonus lines. Hold the gross. Beat the competition, of course, both inside and outside the dealership. Git 'er done and in the books before the month ends.

On the first of the month, it begins all over again. Come the fifth, commissions come out, minus draw, pack, and deductions like health insurance and taxes. You're usually left with a Hershey bar. Not to worry, we'll get it going next month. Of course, if you don't cover the draw, they get rid of you—blow you out.

Finally, you have to deal with CSI. It's what I call "The Kiss-Ass Index," but it really stands for the "Customer Satisfaction Index." Back in the 70s, CSI was created. Some clever Yuppie decided it was possible to make money by having customers rate the businesses they were buying from. Customer Satisfaction Index. It became God to automobile manufacturers and dealerships everywhere.

I personally decided a long time ago that CSI is a false god. It is a manifestation of the Big Lie. The Big Lie is the enemy. The Big Lie is the means by which the collective or the system (whichever way you choose to identify authority) has its way with us.

The Big Lie is the way they beat us.

Think about it. The Big Lie is how people are manipulated, and tricked. The Big Lie is the enemy of our civilization and ultimately our freedom.

With the Big Lie, you can make the world stand on its head. You can make people believe that less is more. You can make people believe that ugly is beautiful. You can make people believe that the planet is heating up, even though it isn't. You can even make people believe   perversion is just an alternative lifestyle.

With the big lie you can even get people to believe that killing babies is okay. Sorry folks I'm digressing a little bit I'm supposed to be talking about cars and their symbiotic relationship to people and our national culture and car wars. Nevertheless, the world of sales and market penetration is also the world of exploitation and manipulation—at the

very least, in so far as people's
perceptions are concerned.

Axiom: Perception is reality. People can
be manipulated by distorted perception.
Or as we say in sales, "Don't sell the steak;
sell the sizzle."

Back to the car wars.

So I didn't feel that I needed any survey to
tell me how satisfied my customers were.
Selling cars is tough business. Whenever a
customer purchases an automobile from
me and drives away, I figure he or she
was 100% satisfied or they wouldn't have
completed the transaction.

I learned very early if people don't like
you, they will not purchase from you. I
also learned that sometimes people feel
remorseful about their decisions. This

usually happens after some time has passed, and something has gone wrong. Whatever the case, the general rule in the business goes like this: "It's the salesman's fault." After all, who ranks highest on the old stink meter up there along with outlaws, lawyers, and politicians? You guessed it—car salesman. Nobody ever believes a car salesman. Our credibility is always nil. People assume we are all liars before they ever set foot on the lot, before they ever even know our name. People are afraid of us. They think we're out to rip them off.

Car salesmen have a different view. We have a saying, "Buyers are liars." The customers *lie* to *us*. Our objective is not to rip them off. Our objective is to get them to buy our car instead of somebody else's. The customer's objective is to get in, get a price, and get away to go and compare it. Both parties are primarily motivated by simple primal fear of making mistakes. The customer doesn't want to get ripped off; the salesman doesn't want to blow the deal.

It's not really as stressful and confrontational as it sounds. In fact, in most cases the sale goes pretty easily. That is, if an experienced professional such as myself is handling the deal. A great car deal is like a great seduction, masterfully controlled to the ultimate satisfaction of both parties.

A great car salesman is a master at reading people. He knows how to schmooze them, how to please them, and how to squeeze them, so they like it. He knows cars for sure, but he also understands that for Americans buying a car is a "Big Deal." Not so much because of the financial aspects involved, but because of the human ego factor.

A person's car is a lot like the clothes they wear. It makes a statement about who they are, and how they present themselves to the world. A good car salesman knows how to "lay just right" with people. He knows how to put them at ease. His confidence and knowledge instills trust. He taps their emotions to build enthusiasm and emotion. Once you've got emotion, you've got two things: One, a deal. Two, gross.

Gross is the term we use to describe the amount of profit on the deal, and car salesmen are paid a percentage of the gross. Therefore, it is very important to us for obvious reasons. When you don't hold gross, but you still make the sale, you get paid a "mini commission." The mini commission is called a "mini deal." A mini deal amounts to a flat $50 to $100 before taxes. It doesn't take a math genius to figure out that it takes a whole lot of mini deals to cover even a very modest rent or mortgage.

Some dealers pay "volume bonuses" to help the situation, but the bottom line is this: Mini deals don't get the job done. What's a fella to do? Answer: Hold Gross.

If you consider the fact that most dealers like to keep at least twice as many salespeople as they need, it is easy to see why most salesmen fail. Those of us who survive can only be described as existentialists. That means we're nuts, gone, stubborn, stupid. Drugs, alcohol, gambling, and carousing are the most common outlets to the endless frustration.

Enough of this heavy stuff. Let's talk cars. Then again, since I'm spilling my guts, I might as well take the time to mention a couple of the urban myths that surround and impede what I do.

First of all there is no such thing as two sets of invoices. So Mr. and Mrs. Customer, stop accusing us of keeping secret cost figures. The automobile business is probably the only retail business on the planet that has exact costs which are easily accessible on the Internet. If you want hidden invoices, try the meat processing industry or the jewelry industry or the recording industry or government procurement.

The second thing is that just because the prices are published on the Internet does not mean that the autos can be purchased at those prices. Funny how the customers always forget that we are in business to make a profit. So stop expecting stupid things to happen. Besides, the Internet buyers always get it wrong anyway. They don't understand things like hold-back, advertising charges, regional incentives, loyalty incentives, or supplier and employee incentives. No matter what you do on the Internet, you still have to end up talking to a sales person. You need our help. You really do. That's what we do! We help people and thereby help ourselves.

I will admit that there are certain types of customer that make salesman want to behave badly or simply run away.

One of the great mysteries of car dealing is, "Where does the elephant go to die? Where does the Hindu go to buy?" Asian buyers are too tough. Europeans are arrogant. Muslims are obnoxious. Real estate salespeople are ruthless. Attorneys are controlling. Celebrities are insufferable. Jewish buyers are all of the above. But you know what? A good car salesman has the knowledge and the skills to handle all these special types of customers. At least, the successful ones do. The truth is, dealing with different kinds of people is the very essence of our business. That's why it's not easy.

We need those people—all of them--"tire kickers, strokers, lookie-loos, moochers, and liars. They are all special. Annoying pains in the ass maybe, but special nevertheless. A really "savvy" salesman allows the customer to think that he is in control all the way until he finds himself driving the car home. Then, only then, does the customer come out of the ether and realize he met up with a salesman., which is what he was looking for in the first place and just didn't know it.

People say and do crazy things, but in the end, they expect to get what they want. We have another saying: "There is an ass for every seat." We try to give them what they want.

In the USA we have all kinds of cars and I'm not just talking brands. We have getaway cars, commuter cars, beaters,

armored cars, taxicabs, jitneys, parade
cars, classic cars, race cars, antique cars,
stock cars, and Indy cars. We have kitty
cars, soapbox derby cars, police cars, fuel
dragsters, snooty cars, Yuppie cars, luxury
cars, pickup trucks, SUVs, jeeps, roller
coaster cars, dune buggies, economy cars
and yes we have yuk... choke... barf...
foreign cars.

We have lots of colorful names for rides,
too. To mention a few and from best to
worst they go like this:

A nice ride is "bitchin'," if you come from
California. Otherwise, it's a "nice ride, nice
wheels, sweet ride, hot wheels, hot Rod,
city cruiser, run about, low rider, leaner,
smooth ride, the old horse and buggy, my
beater, clunker, POS (piece of shit) or
simply "a rat."

Whoever you are, whatever you drive, if
you live in America, you will learn about

the car game. May you all find that deal you are looking for.

As for me, fast Willie? I am just hoping that the government will get out of the car business, and that Cadillac stops worrying about building better BMWs and trucks and goes back to being and building real Cadillacs. Hint to GM: Long, low, wide, solid, fast, imposing, and unmistakably American. The key to blending engineering and art is to embrace an iconic tradition by demonstrating its permanent connection to then, now, and tomorrow.

POP CULTURE, CELEBRITY GLITZ, AND THE STAR SYSTEM

As I stated in the beginning, the under language comes from all over. Yet perhaps, the single greatest force in vernacular creation, as well as confirmation, is video imagery created in film, television, or other broadcasting or distributive purposes.

Hooray for Hollywood , that crazy ballyhooey Hollywood. ("Hooray for Hollywood," Johnny Mercer, 1937)

"LA's got a great big freeway. Put 100 down and buy a car. In a week maybe two they'll make you a star," ("Do You Know the Way to San Jose, " Burt Bacharach and Hal David, 1968.)

We also talked, in the beginning, about winners and losers. If you were born American you are taught to be a winner. Why? Simple -- winners can have it all. The star gets to have his cake and eat it, too.

One picture is worth 1,000 words as the saying goes. For American pop culture and star system, including Hollywood, network and cable TV, radio, print media, and Madison Avenue, that phrase describes the very foundation of their power.

What is the star system and what is a star? We're not talking astronomy and astrophysics here.

A star is a celebrity, a person who is, has been, or just recently become very well-known or famous. There are many ways to become famous. There are many ways

to become a star. It is the symbiotic
relationship between the star and his or
her followers which helps to create under
language, and manufacture new
vernacular.

The invention of the printing press made
Jesus Christ the world's first superstar.
Thereafter, the printed word added in our
heroes who became history's stars.

You know the first ones you encounter as
you grow up. You've got your Bible stars,
like Moses, Sampson, David, Solomon, and
Jesus, Mary, and Joseph.

Along with the bad guys like Lucifer, the
Philistines, the Egyptians, the Sodomites,
the Babylonians, Bathsheba, Queen of
Sheba, Delilah, and don't forget Pontius
Pilate.

After the Bible heroes come the mythological heroes like Hercules, Zeus, and the other Greek gods. And there are Achilles, Hector, and Paris, and of course, Ulysses and Helen of Troy. Then you get more real-life history heroes like Alexander, Caesar, Hannibal, Marc Antony, Cleopatra, Octavian/Augustus, Nero, Caligula, Constantine, and Charlemagne. Then you got more legends like King Arthur and the Knights of the Roundtable, and Roland in the pass.

Then, more real history stars like George Washington, Benedict Arnold, Alexander Hamilton, Andrew Jackson and the real folk heroes like Boone, Crockett, and Bowie.

All of these came before photography. A picture is worth 1,000 words. Photography brought to life -- faraway people in faraway places. The whole second half of the 19th century was

captured in still photography. For the first
time, the images, events, and people of
history could be made available for all to
see.

It got better from there. After print and
photography came moving film and
sound. Radio and TV completed the
picture (no pun intended).

There are many forms of visual media and
the Internet is always growing bigger.
But at the foundation of it all is
Hollywood and the creation of full feature
films. It is the many Stars, past present
and future which power the machine,
which crank up the legends and myths of
our modern times

"What we do in life echoes in eternity,"
says Maximus, hero of the blockbuster
movie *Gladiator*. Those words have never
rung more truly than now in our time.

The words must first be written and then
mixed together with pictures and sound
into moving images so that they can be
seen by other people. Only then can the
myths and legends be set free to spread
out across the world and into the future.

And just as we have seen history and
human activity theatrically captured and
recreated on film, which served to set our
hearts afire, so the images that we create
and send forth now will echo forward
across time to be seen by our near and
distant descendents.

Like the real stars above, the human
Stars serve as markers -- reference points
frozen in time, forever helping us to map
human nature as we go about the
business of evolution. Whenever
somebody does or says or performs in an
extraordinary or superlative manner and

is captured by imagery and sound so that other people are able to view it or hear it and he or she becomes talked about widely, so much that it becomes part of the common knowledge and people remember it. At that moment a Star is born.

When the idea manifests, it can be anything. A certain look he or she has, a way of turning phrases, a quirky difference that stands out, or simply as we say, "He or she has a way about him." A special look, a special sound, which crystallizes the meaning of the idea right into the minds of hundreds and spreads virally to millions, who see it like a beacon and are drawn to it.

And it is the under language which always supports it verbally and visually. The heroes and heroines say the words as only they can say them and we hear it and see it and understand it instantly right to the core of our being.

"Here's to you kid," "Make my day," "Are you talking to me?" "Go for it'." "Yo, Adrian!" "Stella!" "I could've been a contender." "I'll make them an offer they can't refuse." "We might be able to tape the gun behind it." "Nuts!" "You're going down." "Who's going to stop me?" "What did you hear, Shane?" "I heard that you were a low-down Yankee liar." "Prove it." Bang! Pow! Smack! The good guys always win. In the land of E Pluribus Unum (out of many, one). It takes the many to create the one, it takes the one to impact and thereby influence the many. Hence the symbiotic relationship in action.

Stars standout. We recognize them instantly, just like we recognize the message in the vernacular when it's spoken to us. The star is "the real deal." He or she "has IT." The star talks the talk and walks the walk.

The most common theme found throughout American motion pictures is the story containing plenty of macho, bravado, bombast, melodrama, romance, disagreeable bad guys, lots of tits and ass, lots of pyrotechnic stunts, riding, shooting, and driving fast.

Old-fashioned American values are put to the test. The hero is inevitably a down-in-his-luck guy who gets one last chance to make good and makes the most of it. The hard-pressed good guys somehow find a way to win. The bad guys and gals always get what's coming to them. In the end the hero gets the girl rides off into the sunset.

And oh what a girl she is! We like them busty, with long dancer's legs that seemed to go right up to her neck, plus a heart-shaped ass like a Las Vegas stripper. A happy, turned-up face with big eyes and long blond or red hair, but hot, vampy brunettes are always welcome, too. "A wiggle in the walk and a giggle in the talk." Whether she is Betty Boop, Daisy Mae, May West, Wonder Woman, Marilyn Monroe, or just "the girl next door," she is what every red-blooded American boy really wants.

And that's just the easy part.

It turns out that behind all those good looks and sexual magnetism, she is a very complicated girl.

For the male lead you start with a square-jawed hard-muscled, came-up-the-hard-way, but was not marked by it type. Then add in some quiet humility, a fierce sense of justice and fair play, along with silent determination. He is a man of few words or one of erudite precision and he's got a slightly cocky attitude. He's a confident guy. Also he packs a punch like a mule and picks the right time to use it.

Surround him with the right characters
with the right ethnic mix of flavors and
you've got your typical cross-section of
the American group dynamic in action.

How much of our unique lingo comes out
a film? Answer, tons. "Wow, baby you're
looking good today." "We love to see your
work. Beautiful!" "It's a beautiful thing."
"Cut, print! That's a wrap."

"Is it real or is it Memorex?"

The majority of people lead stressful
drudge-filled lives. Why? Because that's
what pays the bills. However, the great
power of moving images is that it permits
the viewer the vicarious experience. In
effect, the viewer is able to experience
hitting the home run in the ninth inning,
or winning the most desirable woman, or
piloting a spaceship to Mars, or any other
experience known to the human

condition. Even the loneliest, most isolated person is not disconnected from the rest of humanity, if he possesses a cable or satellite TV connection. Video imagery provides a sense of inclusion, and that is where the power *really* is.

Yet we must be able to distinguish the real from the illusion. We Americans are in unexplored territory now. We are making it up as we go. We manufacture our own mythology daily. We bend and revise history to suit our own interpretations and arguments. We keep tearing down the old America and replacing it with new iconic forms. Nevertheless, we need to remember where we came from and what the truth really was.

Nowadays, we are bombarded with these symbols and moving images—backed up by carefully crafted and contrived words everywhere we look. We have everybody—from talk-show hosts to political conspirators to social engineers to movie producers and directors to news broadcasters and advertising people—all trying to play with our heads and manipulate us every day.

In spite of all this, certain iconic symbols and character types always persist. This is because we recognize them and we know that they are us. Americans know that there is truth and there is bullshit. And despite the best efforts of the manipulators, we know the difference.

"Don't piss down my back and tell me it's raining." "Don't shine me on." "Don't tread on me."

The Star System permeates our society from top to bottom. It reaches out to us every day in 1,000 different ways. It provides recognition, iconic symbolism, and vicarious experience from a safe vantage point—character revelation or deception or a nagging voice in the back of our heads. It can be informative, manipulative, or escapist. It can result in high art and truth revealed, or serve as an aid to the Big Lie.

It is not a fair system, even though it very much appears that way. It may seem to be about merit, yet it is most definitely premeditated and artificial and specially crafted to elicit the desired effect. It can be about the truth and serve the truth or it can be a lie masquerading as the truth. It is always about a pre-planned outcome.

An integral portion of the Star System is composed of the "Wide World of Sports." In our day and age with widespread satellite media, it is possible for sports celebrities to vie with film celebrities, political celebrities, and other media types for high fame and fortune.

Unlike film, media, and even print, the world of competitive sports has existed much longer. We know from history that athletic competition begin with the Olympic Games and, of course, the Romans held violent games and competitions throughout their Empire. What we are getting at is that the world of sports is a much deeper and older connection to human behavior than the more recent ascension of film and media celebrities. In fact, the sports celebrities go back in time with political celebrities and the two were deeply interconnected.

The Star System requires creative talent and social skills as well as the right appearance to achieve success. The wide world of sports requires physical talent in order to ensure success. In both cases we say you've got to "have what it takes."

The thing about sports is that it is rooted in older, more primitive survival characteristics and behavior. This is because sports games were once used to prepare young men for war, or at least combat. In the beginning, athletic ability was considered a prerequisite for martial training. Look at the way predators train their young.

In our time, athletic competition serves more and more as a profitable psychological replacement for war. There are international competitions, there are inter-state rivalries, there are inter-city rivalries, there are local rivalries, and there are individual rivalries and competitions. Early on, it was about personal combat, tribal combat, mating competition, leadership competition, a safe outlet for the release of testosterone.

Despite the fact that we live in a violent world, it can probably be said that the

great majority of people today do not, in
fact, take part in violent behavior or
actual war. Amateur and professional
sports have provided modern society and
modern citizens with an alternative outlet
to violent behavior and war as well as a
highly profitable area of human endeavor.

"He's got the action. He's got the motion.
Oh yeah, the boy can play.
Dedication, the devotion, turning all the
nighttime into the day." (*Walk of Life*,
Mark Knopfler, 1985)

Every day we talk sports analogies, sports
metaphors, and sports phrases. The
principles of successful athletic
competition are everywhere applied to
our lifestyle; it's almost a kind of national
philosophy.

Every American kid growing up, every businessman or salesman, every person acting on his or her ambitions, every person facing adversities in the course of his or her daily life, profession, or business uses the sports metaphors and analogies.

If you can't score "a knockout," you want to "go the distance." When you get "up to the plate," you want to "step up and get a hit." Or better yet, score "a home run." If you "take your best shot", and swing and miss three times it's a "strike out." You lose. But if you "hang in there," "hang tough," sometimes you can "come from behind," and "pull it out."   If you "get tagged," "get up off the deck," and "come back to win," that is a demonstration of your character.

Every day, we "put on our game face" and "take the field" to take on the opposition. We tried to be great competitors. We practiced our fundamentals. Don't get cute. Don't get fancy. Keep your eye on the ball. Swing the bat straight and level. Study the other guy's moves. Establish his tendencies. Have the countermoves ready. "Grace under pressure." If you "can't move the ball on the ground, drop back and throw deep," or try "the old end around." You get "a seal here and seal there and run to daylight." "Just WIN baby."

Yep the big leagues "separate the men from the boys." The title "coach" is synonymous with the term "mentor." The title "quarterback" is synonymous with "leader." Remember the speech made by Gen. Patton at the beginning of the famous biographical film.

As Americans, we tend to admire and love to make heroes from our winners. Everybody admires the toughest boxer, the coolest quarterback, the strongest running back, the meanest linebacker, the biggest lineman, the clutch hitter, the ace pitcher, and even the best golfer. It's about being the *best*. "Winning isn't everything; it's the only thing."

The great thing about sports stars is that they are the "real deal." They can only get to where they are by "delivering the goods, cutting the muster, making it happen." They can't do it with just their looks, shooting off their mouths, trickery, chicanery, bold lies, or any other form of bullshit. The greatest athletes deliver their greatest performances against their greatest adversaries—when the stakes are at the highest and everything is on the line. It's winner take all—all the money, all the glory, all the fame.

As people, we are the same as everyone
else. Our unique under language provides
separation. Under language reveals the
way in which we are taught to think and
act. This is our edge. It puts us out in front
of the pack. It enables us to bounce back
and overcome the odds. "To play catch up
and come from behind." "To come
through when the chips are down." The
Stars do their thing and shine to light our
way.

THE GALAXY OF AMERICAN OBSCENITY AND PROFANITY

PART I: OBSCENITY

by Prof. Cornelius Holycow Emeritus, American University of Hard Knocks.

Obscenities are as American as anything American can be. You only have to glance at the list to see the high percentage of words and phrases that are not only derisive and vulgar but also totally and unabashedly obscene. The American vernacular, what the author calls "the under language" is loaded with socially taboo terminology. It flows freely around us every day.

Why is this so, and how did it come about
? That is a story 400 years in the making,
involving hundreds of millions.
Therefore, for the sake of brevity, I will
just try to hit a few of the high points.

To probe the galaxy of American
obscenity is to discover and reveal the
most provocative and disturbing secrets
of the vast diversified melting pot that is
the American psyche.

BE WARNED! People reading this
material will disturb and outrage "the
better angels "of your nature. No matter
what part of the genetic spectrum you
come from, this material is upsetting. It is
a shaming feeling of guilt,
embarrassment, and disgust and you may
want to apologize to God for even
knowing about this kind of stuff.

Nevertheless, it's here. It's real. It happens every day, and we are all guilty in some way. (Except for the Saints, but not for the hypocrites who try to pass themselves off as Saints.) Anyway here we go. Hang on this is going to be a rough ride.

Swearing and cursing must have started as soon as our ancestors stepped off the boat. "Shit it's cold here. Damn there's a lot of trees. Holy shit that's a lot of Indians. Damn; we should have brought more men. Damn; we should have brought more beads. Where is all the god-damned gold? They never told us we would have to work so fucking hard."

This kind of talk has been going on for centuries and we have constantly added to it creating an ever-expanding vocabulary of profane lingo. Fast forward to now, and let's take stock of where we are in this regard.

It is the year 2011. And we all live in a
world of shit. First of all, every American
knows "Shit Happens." Then, you have
"good shit and bad shit." "No shit," you
say? Well... listen up." Consider the
connotations the word shit can have and
its impact on society.

"Good shit" is sweet, like money, good
liquor, tobacco, marijuana, cocaine,
heroin, or beautiful women, or most any
form of consumptive, consumable, or
possessable gratification possible.

Bad or "nasty shit" stinks. It stinks
because it means trouble. When we get
into trouble we say, "We are in deep shit."
We usually achieve this by finding ways to
insert our "heads up our asses" and
"Bingo!" There's the shit.

Sometimes we step in it. In America, to metaphorically "step in shit" can be for good or bad. When a guy has good luck we say, "He stepped in shit." Conversely, when a guy has bad luck (usually the result of a bad decision or bad behavior) we say, "He really stepped in shit this time."

Or when really bad mistakes have been made or just discovered, we say, "Now we are really in deep shit," or "The shit is getting so deep a fellow needs and entrenching tool in his back pocket just to get around here." And when bad things overdue finally let go we say, "The shit has hit the fan."

The word Shit comes from way back in the age of sailing ships. "Shite" was the word given to precarious cargo which was stacked on the deck so that it might fall off easily during a storm, and thereby, prevent the ship from rolling over and sinking. Hence the term, "Stacking shite."

Since then, we have created dozens of variations and permutations of the word. Let us name a few examples of good old American verbal diarrhea. Start with "shithead "and go from there. That one is behaving like "a little shit." This one thinks he is a "big shit." He or she thinks "their shit doesn't stink."

Then there is bullshit and the bullshitters. Bullshit is just like rabbitshit , horseshit or malarkey. Bullshit is not ever to be believed. People who succumb to bullshit are considered foolish, squares, gullible, chumps, or strunzes.

Whenever we can no longer tolerate a given situation we say, "I can't stand this shit," or "I've had enough of this shit," or "their shit," or "this shit" or "his or her shit." When we don't buy somebody's story we say, "That's a crock of shit" or "What a crock of shit" or simply, "Bullshit."

When our machines break down we say they "shit the bed" or they"took a shit"

When old guys berate young guys they "get in their shit" and say things like, "What do you know? You were still shitting mustard."

When somebody's "had a few too many" we say they are "shitfaced." When somebody gets something nasty spilled on them we say they are "covered in shit." Ditto for crooked politicians or anybody else busted for some kind of chicanery. And if somebody or something doesn't look to good, we say, "You look like shit."

When we wake up in the morning with a hangover and morning mouth we say, "My mouth tastes like a cat shit in it." When somebody overreacts with a bad temper we say, "Who shit in your cornflakes this morning?"

If we think a person is stupid we say he or she has "shit for brains." Or he or she is just a "dumbshit."

Whenever a person or group of persons confronts, conflicts, or competes with another person or group of persons and really wins out big time and comes out on top and it is done with great gusto and prejudice we say, "They really beat the shit out of him, her, or them."

Whenever person takes over a task from a failed predecessor we say that he or she or they came in and had to "clean up your shit."

Finally, when we feel that all the value or functionality and usefulness have been exhausted in a person or thing we say, "He/she/they/it ain't worth shit." Or that's just a "pile of shit" or "piece of shit" or a "P. O. S."

Orbiting our world of Shit is a moon. It is the Moon of Ass. For obvious reasons, ass is closely related to shit.

In America there is more than enough ass around and we see to its distribution in myriad ways.

Let's start at the bedrock foundation and work our way up.

Asshole is where it all begins. There are 300 million assholes in America and every one of them has an opinion. We have big assholes, little assholes, and regular, everyday assholes. Once we get warmed up, we shorten it up by dropping the holes, and so can more easily describe the specific characteristics of particular *types* of assholes.

You can be just a simple ass or it can be any number of original and more exotic types such as "a bad ass (which is one of the only few good asses), a dumb ass, a stupid ass, an iron ass, a jackass, a horse's ass, a gold-plated ass, a country ass, an ass-wipe, a fine ass, a heart-shaped ass, a black ass, a lily-white ass," or a "good piece or bad piece of ass."

Then there are ways to elaborate on what "ass" can do or receive. Like, "take it up the ass," or you tell somebody to "shove it up his or her ass," or "blow it out their ass "or you will "kick their ass" by administering an "old-fashioned ass-kicking." In the end, we all come to realize that metaphorically or biologically, "Assholes rule this world." Our bosses and leaders prove this every day.

Although the world of Shit and its companion moon, Ass, add some dismal chapters in American profanity and vulgarity they are not nearly the darkest nor most sinister. That title is claimed by the gas giants -- Prejudice and Derision. Here we can find the very roots of ancient and primitive dislikes and hatreds. This is where we find the really nasty disturbing stuff.

This stuff is all from the pulpy area underneath the wholesome dazzle of civilized veneer and the erudite self-congratulation of the social elite. This stuff comes from the old brain as well as old times. It is sort of an anti-reflection of the age-old struggle.

It reveals personal battles, mental battles, and philosophical battles. It's the haves against the have-nots, the advantaged against the disadvantaged, the talented versus the jealous, the greater tribes versus the lesser tribes, the individual versus the collective, us versus them, man versus man -- no holds barred ,no rules, anything goes, win at all costs. To hell with the other guy, damm the consequences, no mercy, it is what it is; the weak versus strong. Winner takes all.

Justice is blind, revenge is sweet, and hard feelings over deep grievances simmer sometimes for centuries. All that stuff has taken root in the national subconscious and is reflected in the under-language as profanity or blasphemy, or racial and ethnic epithets. Each and every one of them has derisive connotations and bad intentions. Yet curiously, not in every case.

Therefore, in order to avoid the glaring horror of the very real extreme nastiness of these words, we shall deal with them from a slightly different perspective. America is known the world over as the Great Melting Pot. We have people from every part of the world, from every nation or tribe and in most cases, in fairly large to very large numbers. In every case, in even that of the original Anglo-Saxons, the new arrivals experienced some form of social, economic, racial, religious, or ethnic persecution.

This work is not intended to offer judgments but to reveal record and catalog the American vernacular and how it is used every day by us. It is the author's sincere hope and wish that nobody takes umbrage or insult or personal offense at the following words and phrases as written down here.

PART 2: ETHNICITY AND RACE

MY BIG FAT-ASS, FULL-OF-SHIT AMERICAN FAMILY
BY Ego Gigante

Start with me. I am a wop. You know a dago, a spaghetti bender, a Guiney, a goombah, a paisan, a greaseball, a mustache. What does all that mean? It means that I am Italian. Not Italian Italian, but Italian American. You know, Sons of Italy, Knights of Columbus, Roman Catholic Church -- lucky people who got to escape from dirt poor war-ravaged Italy to come to America.

Yep that's us. We are here now and glad to be here. We think everybody else should be glad, too. But you know what we say? "There are only two kinds of people in the world: Italian-Americans and people who want to be Italian-American."

Italian-Americans like me are proud to be American. But we guard our Italian heritage jealously and have worked hard to blend in with our new American ways and "it's all good," as my black cousins would say.

The Italian culture advocates a certain zest for life. It should because it took 2,000 years or so to evolve. Here in America, it has taken strong root. You could say that in a way Italy was the world's first melting pot. The ancient Romans established an empire that spread over three continents and so brought slaves from everywhere to work in Italy. Eventually 50% of the population of Italy was made up of slaves.

After the fall of the Roman Empire, the descendents of the slaves mingled with the descendents of the original inhabitants and Bada-bing! You got your modern Italians. Here we are in America and we are back in the melting pot again.

Now some people say bad things about us and others think bad things and some do both. Some people think we are all about thugs and gangsters. Yeah, yeah..., some of us did some of that. So what? Can't let a few bad apples spoil the whole barrel." OK, so I have established the politically incorrect aspects of being derived from Italy. But we need to move on.

My Italian heritage only accounts for half of me.

My mom's side is another story. My mother's people came from Eastern Europe. That means everybody whose name ends in ski, vich, ov, or off. That makes me a hunky which can be Polish, Russian, Czech, Serbian, Bulgarian, Romanian, or Hungarian. Of course the

Romanians are already half-and-half like me.

Being a hunky has its downsides. To start with, everybody likes to go around telling jokes about us. You know dumb Polak this, dumb hunky that. In rundown lingo, that makes me half-greasy, oversexed, criminally-inclined, cement-loving wop and half dumber than a bag of hammers cousin to a moron hunky.

That is only a small percentage of good old American prejudiced bigoted terminology. Not to worry, now comes my extended family. That would be the uncles and aunts and cousins and in-laws and cousins and in-laws of the in-laws. Now as they used to say in the 60s, "We're going to let it all hang out."

Let's see, how about the Anglo-Saxons go first since they got here first (except for

Columbus and Cabot, two guys from Genoa). That would be my uncle John was married to my father's sister.

My uncle John is always touting his English bloodlines and bragging about how the white Anglo-Saxon Protestants founded the country and still control everything to this day. This, even though he chose to marry into our extremely diversified multi-ethnic family and sired two of my half-breed cousins. It is uncle John's long-considered attitude that, except for other Nordic Protestant Europeans, the rest of us are all part of what was once known as the 'White Man's Burden." Of course this makes him the most prominent bigoted and prejudiced hypocrite in the family.

His two best friends are my father's other sister's husband, Pete and his brother, Stush -- both Polish. They all work together and all you hear from them is

Polak, this Polak that. Pete and Stush mainly just encourage him to "shut the fuck up" because it's against the law to spread stupidity.

There's more. Uncle John's brother, Bobby, who shares most of Uncle John's views, has made his own far more extensive editions of the family's diversification. You see, Bobby has three wives from three different races, with kids.

Colleen is his first wife's name. Colleen is Irish. Bobby and Colleen proved beyond a doubt that the Irish and English still hate each other with gusto. Bobby has always had a natural attraction for dark hair and dark skin. Colleen has dark hair and swarthy skin.

Bobby met Leticia when she was working at a pancake house. But of course, Latisha

is black all over -- eyes, hair, and skin.
Pure brown sugar. It wasn't long before
Bobby moves in with her. He gave her two
kids and then married her.

Of course, he never bothered to get
divorced. Instead, he split his time
between the two wives living at both
houses and raising both families. But it
doesn't end there. Yolanda was his first
wife's babysitter and she didn't have a
green card but she hit it right off with
Bobby. Bada-bing! You've got your
number three wife. Still no divorces.

So how does a guy not from Utah or Saudi
Arabia get away with that? Simple, he
just explained to each of them that if they
complained to the law he would shoot all
three of them. They all seem quite content
with the arrangement. At least they all
show up at the holiday and family
gatherings.

The family has other far-flung branches.
My uncle Nick lives in New Jersey. The
old-timers used to call Nick "The Terrible
Turk" because he had such a bad temper
and they made fun of him because his skin
was so black.

He is married to Connie, a fiery redheaded Irish girl. His sons, my cousins,
are as black as him in spite of their fair-
skinned mother. Each of them married
first-generation girls from the
subcontinent. One from India, a Hindu,
and the other from Pakistan, a Muslim.

My grandmother's first cousin was called
"Mary the Syrian" and she moved to
California. She married a Russian guy.
My grandmother's sister's daughters (also
from California) married outside the lines,
too -- one to Sam, who is Lebanese, and
another to Lashon (you can guess) and

another to a Swedish rancher from
Oregon named Torger. My Aunt
Catherine's son, Matthew (again from
California) married a guy named Bruce,
from Frisco.

Farthest away, my grandfather's youngest
sister in Sicily married a guy who couldn't
get into the states and ended up in
Buenos Aires. Their daughter married a
rich Mexican descended from Santa Anna
himself and ended up living in South
Florida, where her kids married Cuban-
Americans.

Finally, my cousin Rocky married a
Korean girl he met while stationed over
there, and his brother, Carmen, married a
Japanese girl from Okinawa. They both
settled in Hawaii after, they got out of the
service. Their kids each married a
Filipino, an Australian, and a California
Okie from Barstow named Terry, and he
claims to be half Native American.

When we held a 10-year family reunion last summer we had to pay the city for using up half of North Park and crowding out the local residents. It looked like a cross between a union meeting, a special sessions of the United Nations, or a Democratic Party caucus.

So there you have it.

My big, fat-ass, full-of-shit, All-American, extended family. Oh, wait!

I forgot the Jews and the Krauts. My wife is German and Irish so that takes care of the Germans. And my mother's Hungarian grandmother, who never made it across the pond, was a Viennese Jewess. So that's it. Look at what we are. We've got Anglo-Saxons, Italians, Celts, Hispanics, Slavs, Africans, Arabs, Sub-continentals, Asians, Australians, Jews, and Gays. All intermarried and mixed up over just three generations.

In private company, we refer to ourselves
and call each other every degrading,
bigoted, racial ethnic slur collected over
400 years.

We say words like wop, dago, greaseball,
wog, kike, nigger, chink, kraut, polak, dot-
head, faggot, eggplant, spic, redneck, as
pre-faces to words like asshole, shithead,
dumb ass, moron, Princess, beauty queen,
prima donna, and pendejo.

All of it is in jest, and all is kept strictly
within the family. Yet somehow, we don't
feel insulted or personally hurt by it
because we are a family and we have
drawn all the poison out of the words for
each other. We don't say that stuff
outside the family. People would not
understand. Rather, *some* people might
not get it.

There are lots of people whose extended families are similar to ours. Our professions and our politics are as diverse as our backgrounds. But when we hold the reunions everybody has a good time. We are a family of Americans and we all speak the same lingo. We really do understand eachother.

PART THREE: Sex - ASS CONNECTED TO ID BELT

Like the asteroid belt, the never ending variety of American sexual obscenities, perversions, and deviance spreads out, incorporating elements of all the other classifications. If it is not derogatory, racial, ethnic, scatological, or religious, it is sexual.

It is a generally-held belief in America, since the very earliest times, that the ultimate source of evil is the devil. You know... *Old Scratch*, L. Diablo,

Beelzebub... put simply, Satan. The devil figures mightily in the mythology of human sexuality. We know he has a long schlong, and we know he likes the girls. He is the great liar and the great seducer.

He seduced Eve to get us thrown out of the Garden of Eden. Adam was the first cuckold (or strunze if you prefer) . Then the devil created Lilith in order to seduce Adam. Bingo the archetype bimbo was born. Once out of the garden, human sexuality offered almost unlimited possibilities for linguistic development.

All of the scientific, socially, and politically correct descriptions of human sexual activity can be found in the average dictionary.

The act of procreation is called "intercourse, coitus, carnal knowledge, marital consummation, impregnation, or gently and acceptably, making love." In America, it is generally referred to as doing it, going all the way, having relations, seeing somebody, sleeping with somebody, having an affair, hanky-panky, or simply fooling around. Those are all soft euphemisms.

The correct academic terms like heterosexual and homosexual describe certain aspects of preference. Other terms like fellatio, cunnilingus, sodomy, bestiality, fetishism, sadism, masochism, and orgy participant describe specific forms of sexual activity.

But the Father of Lies (the Great Seducer, Old Scratch, yadda, yadda) inspired us to create simpler and far more colorful and descriptive terminology. Simply put:

The Devil created the planet Fuck and made himself King. That is where all the

really wild stuff happens. Planet Fuck is a
state of mind and has its own language.
One of the ways that Old Scratch gets his
rocks off was to twist the words around
like he always does. Turning them into
de-rogs and dis-in terminology. What do I
mean by that?

The devil took the verb "to fuck." which in
itself is the number one crude word
which we use to describe the physical act
of love and procreation. and used it to
spawn and spinoff dozens of negative,
violent, degrading, or otherwise profane
remarks.

Let us start off with "fuck you" and just let
it run -- "fuck off," "fuckhead," "fucking
asshole," "fucking idiot,""fuckface,"
"fucking douchebag," "fucking illiterate,'"
starting to get the idea? Then there is the
all-time greatest and most potent --
"mother fucker."

There is lots of simple stuff such as "Fuck, no," "Fuck, yes," or "Fucking - A," "Get the fuck out," "No fucking way," "Your're fucking crazy," "That's a fucking crock of shit," "He is going to kick your fucking ass," "stupid fuck," "fucktard," "assfuck," "fuckbrain," "fucking cheating whore," "fucking two-timer," "fucking rat bastard."

Did any of those de-rogs even hint at sexual content? Well I suppose if you were to take "mother fucker" literally. But basically, these terms are all commonly used putdowns. They are solidly part of the "under-language." Of course they are most often only used in carefully chosen relaxed company, behind the scenes (and especially behind bars). That is Old Scratch in action, always twisting things.

It continues with the other common sexual obscenities. Along with the verb "fuck" comes the other verb "suck," which of course, is commonly associated with the proper body parts such as the penis, vagina, anus, head, mouth, and lips.

In the vernacular, these are transposed into cock, dick, pussy, cunt, ass, bunghole, backdoor, etc. etc. From there colorful words morph into cocksucker, muff-diver, cunt-eater, pussyface, rug-muncher, lapper, fudge packer, and peter puffer. The meanings are always twisted like a pretzel.

A "cocksucker" is a person who performs a sexual act on a man. They provide "blow-jobs." A woman is called a fellatrix in "haute couture" lingo. But on the street, a "cocksucker" is either a low-class tramp female, a gay male, or just a no-good son-of-a-bitch.

A "lapper' is a man, but a "rug-muncher,"
a gay female. A lesbian with masculine
tendencies becomes a "dyke" or a "butch."
A "faggot" describes a gay male, but
"queer" in gentler times. In history, they
were the most reviled perverts. In the
present day, homosexuals are making
their greatest efforts towards
empowerment since before the "nuking"
of Sodom and Gomorrah.

Sexual de-rogs also imply defiance in
many forms.

For instance the phrase "suck my dick" or
"blow me" sounds sexual. But in fact its
real meaning is closer to "Hell no," with
great prejudice. The phrase is much
stronger than "eat me," "bite me," or "I've
got your [bleep whatever] right here," all
of this while grabbing or pointing to your
crotch.

Calling a woman or a man a "cunt" means she or he is in fact some sort of unsavory, hard to handle, shrewish, and generally distasteful to deal with "bitch."

Goes back to the old joke [chauvinist joke that is] about the kid in school who keeps hearing the words "cunt" and "pussy" used frequently by the other boys, but he is too embarrassed to admit that he doesn't know just exactly what the words mean. So he goes to his father asks, "Dad, what is the meaning of the words and what is the difference?"

Good old dad promptly reaches under his chair and produces a girlie magazine featuring a frontal nude foldout of an attractive young woman. He then takes a marker pen and circles the woman's female genitalia. Then he tells the boy, "Everything inside the circle is a pussy;

everything outside the circle is a cunt."
Again, it is the word-twisting meaning
that matters.

Consider the word "pussy." In the under-
language, the word refers to the female
genitalia with regard to its softness, both
physically and metaphorically. However,
its use as a sexual putdown is
overwhelmingly intended to point out
weakness in the face of adversity or
intimidation. Be it physical violence or
social or political courage "pussies" are
cowards who can't handle pressure in any
form.

The word "chump" is used to describe
someone who is not only a pussy, but also
stupid. Calling someone "yellow" or
"chicken shit" amounts to much the same
thing. But it lacks the degradation that the
sexual twist imparts to the insult.

The last group of sexual de-rogs is, of course, the anal references, which are equal in crudity to any of the other forms. It all seems to be rooted in the most primitive impulses of the American heterosexual male.

The American male is taught to reject any form of submission, or physical penetration by another male. Hence, you have your common homophobia or rejection of homosexuals to the point of violence. Since the days of Sodom and Gomorrah, "peter puffing fudge packers" who "take it up the ass" have been considered an anathema to healthy normal guys everywhere. At least until recently.

If you want to throw out the meanest, lowest, nastiest sexual de-rog possible, you would have to describe your target as "a cock-sucking, pussy, who takes it up the ass." Insults involving talk of anal penetration are not necessarily gay bashing in their intent. They are more about male heteros subconscious fears. Also, gay males, by their very essence, tend to leave themselves open [no pun intended] to such castigation.

That about wraps up this essay on the galaxy of American profanity and obscenity. I sincerely apologize if I missed anything important that should have been included. I realize that I failed to include or deal with religious obscenities in the main text. This is because I deliberately saved it for last.

Religious obscenities are not sexually based, nor are they related to other bodily centered terms as in the world of Shit and the Moon of Ass. By religious obscenities I mean words and phrases like "God damn" this, and "God damn" that and taking the Lord's name in vain by exclaiming, "Jesus Christ!" this, or "Jesus

Christ!" that every time one of life's little
adversities or surprises pop up.

We seem to use religious obscenities at
the least as much as the others in
everyday life. That's where it ties into my
"Old Scratch" theory. All of the profanity
and obscenity "the Galaxy" has its roots in
hate. Old festering, rotting hate that
never dies. Isn't that what the devil is all
about? Hatred of men, hatred of women,
hatred of nations and tribes, hatred of all
beauty and all good, hatred of grace,
hatred of God.

And that is where I want to leave it. I
think we as people need to take the
blame. We find it oh so easy to indulge in
such words. But then, doesn't sin always
come easy? Easy money, easy women,
easy lives, easy way out. Even as we
humbly accept blame, we can perhaps
find solace in the fact that some power far
older and far more clever and knowing

than us is responsible. Atheists and psychologists would say that is a copout.

Most of human literature has been dedicated to the study and revelation of the duality of basic human nature. 5,000 years of history have proven that they can't be preached away or legislated away. It can be killed, but even that hasn't stopped it. The natural human tendency and propensity to curse and cuss can't be stopped. Like... "Shit happens." If God is watching and judging, we better hope that he understands. Otherwise, we are all "fucked!"

WAR

The truth about Americans in war is that Americans like to fight. George S. Patton, one of our famous generals, said it, "All real Americans love the sting of battle."

The way Americans look at it war is as an occurrence or outbreak of evil in the world so reprehensible that *our boys* have to *step in* and *put things right*. Whenever possible, Americans like to *settle their differences, man to man*. In war, we tend to see ourselves or at least our side as *the good guys*. And everybody knows the *guys in the white hats always win*. But we're getting ahead of ourselves; "white hats" is a western theme to be covered later.

War, however, is probably the most consistent and deeply-ingrained theme in the American experience. It is wound and bound tightly throughout American history. Like Ancient Rome, the American people were weaned on war. Today we are the world's superpower, not without serious challengers, but definitely still preeminent. This was not always so.

War began in America the moment our forefathers stepped off the boat. First, we warred against the Native American Indians for possession of the land. The conflict with them ran continuously from the very beginning, until the end of the 19th century when the last belligerent resistance was wiped out.

 Much has been written and said about the Indian wars. We now look back with guilt and regret and disgust upon our ancestors" struggles with the Native Americans. Modern pundits have labeled the whole thing as deliberate genocide. It was a part of the dark side of American history, another long, dirty chapter in the annals of man's cruelty to man.

But it is wrong to judge history by the smug, comfortable moral condescension of our supposedly enlightened times. We have created a whole vernacular to describe it better and in the language of those who lived it.

First of all, *it takes two to tango*. There can't be a fight or war without two parties involved. It wasn't that people just came here to kill the natives so they could take over. Things happened. People reacted. Things got out of control. The new colonists and settlers were not the most enlightened people in the world.

The settlers needed land. The English royalty were looking for profit and exploitation. There was fur and timber from the virgin forest, crops like cotton, tobacco, corn and wheat from the rich virgin soil. There was wealth and geopolitical power to the British Crown and plenty of room to grow for the hard-pressed disadvantaged populations of Europe. There was opportunity in America for the bold, the ambitious, and the daring.

The trouble was that the eastern Indian tribes were populous and well organized—on the verge of a form of nationhood themselves --tribes like the Algonquin, Huron, Iroquois, Ottawa, Mohawk, Mohican, Narragansett, Manhattan, Cherokee, and Seminole. This is just to name a few. In the beginning, there was some resistance but there were also budding friendships and good relations and feelings.

That is how we acquired our first true American holiday. The fall harvest festival has ever since been known as *Thanksgiving*. Today the ever-present politically correct social engineers have converted it into "Turkey Day," a gluttonous drunken football-obsessed, long weekend. Too bad.

If things had been left *well enough alone* there's no telling how the first settlers and colonists might have worked it all out. But other political events were happening that would change American relationships with the Natives forever.

England and France, the superpowers of their time, were engaged in War in Europe, Asia, India, and North America. The seven years war in Europe brought the French and Indian wars to North America. Indian tribes divided and lined up with either the French or the British and the great tribes fought each other as well as the white men.

The settlers were caught in the middle and things got *real ugly* after that. The British and French military taught and encouraged taking of *scalps* as war souvenirs and body count. The spreading atrocities colored and prejudiced the two races against each other forever after.

The only good Indian is a dead Indian. Filthy murdering bloodthirsty devils. Red-skinned savages. Things like tomahawks and wampum belts entered into the legend of the frontier.

The outcome is in the history books.

But individual people lived it one day at a time *up close and personal.* If you were to be transported back in time to be confronted by a war party of very formidable redskin braves bent on *lifting your hair* and burning the house that you built with your own hands one stinking tree at a time, what would you do? Maybe *shoot first and ask questions later?*

What the Indian wars did for the American psyche was to introduce the concept of "*total war.*" War without Mercy. War waged against both the combatants and noncombatants. War against the enemies substance, his crops, his animals, and his economy.

After fighting French and Indians, Americans turned their martial inclinations on their British rulers. The War of Independence brought the next great theme to the American experience.

The *War of Independence* was about freedom. The discovery of the New World had always been about profit and exploitation because of the availability of great space and resources. This naturally led to greater freedoms. There was no way that the self-sacrificing courageous and ambitious dwellers of the new colonies were going to allow a bunch of stuffy, condescending, arrogant, greedy aristocrats *call all the shots* from across the ocean. So, the Revolutionary War became a war for freedom and against tyranny—a righteous mission, worthy of the risk and sacrifice.

"Give me liberty or give me death." "No taxation without representation." "All men are created equal, and are born with inalienable rights," with the main right being the right to break the bonds of tyranny with violence.

To this end Americans were willing to pledge to each other, "their lives, their fortunes, and their sacred honor." *To the death.* So be it.

Fighting for freedom made war a holy cause. The War of Independence gave us names and phrases that will last forever: "The midnight ride of Paul Revere," "One if by land; two if by sea, ""The embattled farmers stood at the bridge of Concorde and fired the shot heard round the world." The stand at Bunker Hill. Washington's crossing of the Delaware on Christmas Eve and the route of the Hessian mercenaries at Trenton...

There was the winter at Valley Forge. *Poor Richard's Almanac* by Benjamin Franklin (more affectionately known as "Benny F"). *Common Sense* by Thomas Paine. *The Declaration of Independence* by Thomas Jefferson and Benny F.

There was Fort Ticonderoga and the Green Mountain Boys. Benedict Arnold and Nathan Hale. Francis Marion, the Swamp Fox. John Paul Jones from the deck of the sinking Bonhomme Richard. "I have not yet begun to fight." There was a new flag of 13 stars and 13 stripes—a *baker's dozen.* "Don't tread on me," it said. Yankee Doodle Dandy and then Yorktown, the Preamble to the Constitution: "We the people of the United States."

Okay now we were a nation—one people, one flag, except for the slaves. But we were not done with war. No way! No, sir!

We were just getting started.

The founding fathers and the framers of the Constitution were obsessed with Roman history. They weren't interested in copying England with its two-tier parliamentary system, supporting a vestigial monarchy, which they viewed as a well-stacked deck in favor of royalty, wealth, power, and privilege.

Instead, they focused on the institutional structure of the ancient Roman Republic and created the world's first constitutional republic based on the Federation of Independent States.

But the war experience wasn't going end there.

Just like the roman republic it was modeled after, the new nation soon found itself embroiled in war after war after war.

In 1789, the same year the US Constitution was written and ratified, Britain was just beginning her twenty-year war with revolutionary and Napoleonic France. During this time, France and Britain stepped on our toes hard.

Our first foreign war was the Quasi War with France, which was primarily a trade war fought at sea. That was how the United States Navy got started. We needed warships to protect our overseas trade. That is when we constructed our first generation of sailing warships the famous frigates Philadelphia, President, Chesapeake, Essex, United States, and the USS Constitution better known to history as Old Ironsides.

The new ships gave the French such a rough time that when Napoleon Bonaparte took over, he wanted to bury the hatchet. Napoleon needed money for his own wars so he sold us Louisiana along with New Orleans and the Great Plains from the lakes to the Pacific Northwest shore. The purchase cost 3 million *bucks*. Hell of a *good deal*. Not quite as good as the Dutch buying New Amsterdam (Manhattan) for twenty-four bucks worth of beads. But hell yes, we took the deal.

Right about then, we ran into the Barbary Pirates. Those early *towel heads* liked to snatch our ships and keep them along with their cargoes, enslave the crews, and ransom the officers or any passengers of wealthy class. Of course white-skinned females brought the highest prices in the slave markets. That's right; Americans were not the only people engaging in slavery at that time. Hell, we didn't even invent the institution.

Anyway, our engagement with the Barbary Pirates helped train up the navy for the coming conflict with England. The young Marine Corps got its first really good ink when they marched along the African coast and fought on the shores of Tripoli.

"Millions for defense but not one cent for tribute" was actually coined by Robert

Goodloe Harper at the beginning of the Quasi naval War with France. The French were trying to put the squeeze on us. The pirates wanted to be paid off, too. In the end, we paid them both with cannonballs.

Now we were ready for the British, or so we thought. The War of 1812 was basically an economic war. It was also about teaching the powerful British bullies to give us some respect.

For the most part we got the worst of it. We tried to invade Canada and promptly got our tails whipped. The British fleet blockaded our coasts and choked off our trade. Then they proceeded to burn Washington. However we got our respect.

Our new frigates proved themselves superior in battle. Naval victories achieved on Lake Ticonderoga and Lake Erie gave us control of the Great Lakes "we have met the enemy and they are ours" Detroit and Chicago became American.

Two weeks after the Treaty of Ghent, Andy Jackson gave the British Army *a lickin'* at the battle of New Orleans. "We fired our guns and the British kept a'comin. There wasn't nigh as many as there was a while ago. We fired once more and they began to runnin' down the Mississippi to the Gulf of Mexico." (Jimmy Driftwood, 1959)

The war of 1812 gave us the story of *The Man without a Country*. It also gave us the *Star-Spangled Banner*, probably the most martial national anthem of all the great nations.

We weren't done with war yet not by a long shot.

During all this time the Indian wars crackled on. Andy Jackson went to Florida and fought the Seminole Indians for seven long years. The Cherokee tribe was forced out of the Southern Appalachian following "The Trail of Tears" to the new reservations in Oklahoma.

In the northwest there was war with Tecumseh and his Indian Federation. There was the Battle of Tippecanoe, and General "Mad" Anthony Wayne marched through Ohio, Michigan, Indiana and Illinois. The Indians left; their names remain.

But there were still new wars to look forward to. A lot of Americans were migrating into Texas, "*Gone to Texas*," was the saying. These were ambitious and adventurous men—men like Stephen Austin, Sam Houston; Jim Bowie, along with his famous knife; and Davy Crockett, wearing his coonskin cap.

The English-speaking American frontiersman did not like living under Spanish style dictatorship. So they started their own country—Texas, the Lone Star. They had their own army, the Texas Rangers, and their own martyrs *"Remember the Alamo "*where Col. William B. Travis, Jim Bowie, and Davy Crockett were massacred along with about 180 men.

Sam Houston and his boys put things right at the battle of San Jacinto and Texas became an independent nation for 10 years.

When Texas applied for entrance into the Union, Santa Anna didn't like it. Hell he couldn't even beat Texas. How on *God's green earth* did he think he could take on the United States? The next thing you know, New Mexico, Arizona, Colorado, Utah, Nevada, and California became part of the Union.

The young American nation quickly mobilized armies and fleets and sent those thousands of miles to invade Mexico, capture Mexico City, and seize California.

The Marines got to add, "From the halls Montezuma," to their hymn. Up to this point, Americans kind of liked this war stuff.

Unfortunately, the diseased institution of slavery was dividing the nation, and spawning hatreds that still last to this day. In places like Kansas and Missouri, and at Harpers Ferry Virginia, Civil War had already begun.

The real trouble came down in 1861. Abraham Lincoln was elected the president and the southern states seceded from the union to form the Confederate States of America.

In four bloody horrible years America invented modern war.

We learned to wage continuous industrial war, every day, in every place possible until the bitter end. Brother fought brother; father fought son; whole cities were leveled; whole populations starved, displaced, and their properties destroyed or confiscated. Death, disease, and hate permeated the land.

The Union was saved. The slaves were freed.

But Americans didn't love war so much now.

Civil War gave us many new names and terms, like Honest Abe, Uncle Tom, blockade runner, ironclads, monitors, submarines, mines, torpedoes, Gatling gun, Dahlgren gun, mini balls, and trench warfare.

"There is Jackson standing like a stone wall," said General Bernard E. Bee.

When asked how he was able t win so many victories, Nathan Bedford Forest said, "I just get there first with the most."

The North adopted the Anaconda Plan. The intention was to blockade the South with the Navy and take control of the Mississippi with the Army.

It wasn't easy.

The American fleet was old and decrepit. The rebels had seized Norfolk Navy Yard and converted the frigate USS Merrimack into the CSS Virginia, one of the world's first ironclads. Their intention was to use her to break the federal blockade. Fortunately, *Yankee Ingenuity* provided the answer in the form of the USS Monitor, an ironclad design by John Ericsson.

In the western theater, Confederates fortified the city of Vicksburg. For two years, battle raged around Vicksburg for control of the Mississippi. The citizens of Mississippi collected iron for the CSS Arkansas, and Ulysses S. Grant became known as "Unconditional Surrender "Grant. Adm. Farragut exclaimed, "Damn the torpedoes, full speed ahead," as he ran past the forts in Mobile Bay.

In the East, the Army of Northern Virginia defeated the Army of the Potomac in battle after battle. The Confederates won at Manassas, at Fredericksburg, and at Chancellorsville. The Union won at Antietam and at Gettysburg." Let us cross over the river, and rest under the shade of trees," said Stonewall Jackson before he died. "Wherever (Gen.) Lee goes there you will go also," Ulysses S. Grant ordered General George G. Meade.

Back in the West the Chickamauga River became known as the bloody Chickamauga or The River of Death. Afterwards followed the battle above the clouds and the Army of the Cumberland assaulted Lookout Mountain. "War is hell," said Sherman, and "...I can make Georgia howl!"

The Battle of Gettysburg was won and Vicksburg surrendered on the same day. The Gettysburg address was Lincoln's greatest speech. At Cold Harbor, 7,000 Americans were killed in 30 minutes. At

St. Petersburg, two American armies lived
in the trenches for six months. At
Appomattox Courthouse, Gen. Grant
showed mercy for the first time.

"Strike the tent," Lee murmured and died.
"Mine eyes have seen the glory," "Yes
we'll gather round the flag boys, we'll
gather round the flag," "Look away
Dixieland." "Thus die tyrants," said John
Wilkes Booth.

Yes, we learned too much about war
during the Civil War and too much about
suffering. But, "...we can never hallow this
ground... for those who gave the last full
measure of devotion." War is killing. We
got real good at it. But we would get
better still.

The Indian wars raged on." Long Hair,
Gen. George Armstrong Custer, was the
"Son of the Morning Star." "Onward to the
Little Big Horn and glory." "You go down

there, General, if you got the nerve," said
the title character in Thomas Berger's
Little Big Man.

Near the end of the 19th century, America
was bursting with industrial might and
imperialistic zeal. What we needed was,
"A splendid little war." "Remember the
Maine! "was the battle cry of 1898.

Actually, the U. S. S. Maine sank because
of a spontaneous coal bunker explosion, a
common occurrence on steamships in
those days. It really didn't matter. We
were looking for an excuse.

"The Galleons of Spain Off the East Coast"
ran the headlines of the yellow press.
Teddy Roosevelt and the Roughriders
charged up San Juan Hill and American
soldiers got to meet Ms. Malaria and Ms.
Typhoid, too.

But the Navy won the war "You may fire when ready, Gridley," said Commodore Dewey. In three hours, 500 years of Spanish colonialism came to an end. Now America had the responsibility of new colonies and protectorates in the Philippines and Puerto Rico.

Too bad the Filipinos didn't see it that way. The Philippine insurgency raged for years. It was responsible for the invention of the model 1911 45-caliber Colt automatic pistol. The Spanish-American war helped sweep Teddy Roosevelt into the presidency. But it also created the big navy lobby and reinforced the Big Gun Club.

Teddy built the Great White Fleet and sent it around the world to carry the Big Stick. Gunboat Diplomacy created the nation of Panama. Roosevelt said, "I took the Canal Zone." He then proceeded to dig mud and make war on the mosquitoes.

In total, it could probably be said that the Spanish-American war served to provide a foundation for what is today known as the military-industrial establishment.

The Philippine insurrection was the first modern insurgency fought by the U.S. Army. But, it was by no means our first experience in guerrilla warfare. The long drawn-out war on the frontier with the Indians provided that experience. Nevertheless, the Philippine insurrection was a long agony for the U.S. Army.

Across the Atlantic, the competition between England and Germany stimulated a battleship building spree here in America, in order to match the growing naval power of Europe and Japan. This was good for our economy as well as our Navy.

During the same time, a famous bandito down in Mexico figured he didn't have to, "Show us any stinking badges." So we sent Black Jack Pershing down there to chase him and his boys around for a while.

Pancho Villa was wanted dead or alive, and like Geronimo, he led our boys on a merry chase all over the Southwest. We never caught him. It was good preparation for next up in our ongoing Roman parade of wars.

World War I had been raging in Europe since August 1914. The Western powers—mainly England, France, and Russia—were really "going at it" with the Central Powers—the German and Austrian empires. Americans tended to sympathize with the allies, but that was about as far as it went. Nobody at home wanted America to get involved in the war.

Trouble was that the Kaiser and his arrogant bastard Prussian officer corps tried to achieve victory by letting their U-boats attack ships without warning. This tactic was considered dastardly and reprehensible by the outmoded leftover 19th-century morality of the time.

The Germans were actually ahead of their time. The poor dumb "Kraut Bastards" just didn't get it. Their precocious military insight only served to bring them into moral conflict with American public opinion. The average American had never heard of Field Marshal von Clausewitz and his famous quote, "War is an extension of politics by other means." To Americans, sneaking up on helpless civilian merchantmen cast the Germans as the bad guys.

Woodrow Wilson who had campaigned on the slogan, "He kept us out of war," now called for America to enter the fight in order to "make the world safe for democracy." Americans didn't know Von Clausewitz. We were more like "an eye for an eye" or "we know a skunk when we smell one."

So, in 1917 Black Jack Pershing had to forget about Pancho Villa and take our boys—the Doughboys—over there. "And we won't come back till it's over, over there."

When they weren't fighting and dying in the trenches, our boys had a pretty good time in France. They learned excellent French like, "Cherchez la femme (look for the woman), and voulez vous mademoiselle and oo la la." They also learned to appreciate wine so much, that some of the guys from California went home and planted vineyards.

World War I gave us lots of new stuff like Thompson submachine guns, Browning automatic rifles, four stack destroyers, sonar and depth charges, Woozlefinches (14 inch naval guns mounted on rail cars), airships, airplanes, and bombers.

The Marines got a new nickname to add to "Leathernecks." The Germans called them Teufel-Hundes or Devil Dogs after the battle of the beautiful wood.

Capt. Eddie Rickenbacker became America's first flying ace. A farm boy from Tennessee, Alvin York single-handedly killed about 150 Germans and captured another 300 more in one day. They gave him the Medal of Honor and Gary Cooper immortalized him forever in film in the movie *Sergeant York.*

Other than the new gadgets, and the new names, and new heroes, America didn't get much out of World War I, except the flu. For the first time since 1865 Americans had had enough of war. It was time to celebrate the peace. The boys came home. The army was immobilized. The Washington Naval Treaty clipped the wings of the Navy, and the navy clipped the wings of Billy Mitchell.

"Happy days are here again" was the song sung in celebration of the end of the war. The Republicans, Warren Harding won the presidency on the platform, "Back to Normalcy," whatever normalcy was.

The time between the two world wars was one of the most peaceful times in American history. The Marines were called upon to intervene in some of the banana republics. Other than that, Americans were mostly occupied with trying to defy prohibition and get rich at the same time by hook or crook.

The roaring 20s were upon us. Everybody wanted to "get lucky with Lindy" and go to "speakeasies" and go to baseball games and watch the "Sultan of Swat" smack balls over the fence.

Jack Dempsey was knocking everybody out until the "fighting Marine" Jean Tunney gave him a boxing lesson. Everybody knows the party ended in 1929.

Everybody thinks that FDR led America out the depression with the New Deal.

Nothing could be farther from the truth.

The truth was that American industry didn't get going strong again until the London Naval Treaty expired in 1936.

Across the Atlantic and Pacific we could see it coming again. We suddenly needed battleships, aircraft carriers, submarines, tanks, trucks, guns, ammo, fighters, bombers, and bombs. That's what pulled us out of the depression.

World War II was the perfect war at the perfect time. We were righteous. The other side was clearly evil. Also we just happened to possess the greatest industrial plant the world had ever seen. And we had the GIs, products of the greatest generation.

Right up to the start, Americans were very antiwar. But the enemy made it easy. The Germans were sinking our ships again and the Japanese were killing everything in sight in China. In truth, the Axis powers were compelled to attack us because we helped the British in the Atlantic and we choked off Japan's oil and scrap iron pipeline in the Pacific.

After Pearl Harbor, that didn't matter. All that mattered was that they started shooting first. The Japanese provided extreme motivation by choosing surprise attack.

Like the Germans in World War I surprise attack was militarily correct but strategically unsound because of the moral impetus generated in American public opinion. In short it pissed off the guy in the street.

Americans believed then and still believe today that the human race, in general, and most people in particular, are basically good. War, however, is generally regarded as an aberrant outbreak of evil like the eruption of plague or epidemic. It must therefore be met with righteous unrelenting violence until all resistance is crushed a' la the Civil War.

World War II met all requirements. It provided America with the ultimate definitive war experience. Unlike the Civil War, which had divided us, World War II united us in a way that has never happened before or since.

It was documented on film. It has been reenacted artistically in literature and on stage and in Hollywood in all its myriad perspectives, until it has been ingrained in every American born since.

If war is the greatest theme in the American experience (and it truly is), then it also expressed America's feelings like no other event in national memory. And that's saying a lot because all the way up to then, and since then, war has remained an indelible constant in American history.

Just like in World War I, we invented all kinds of neat new stuff, like radar and radar-controlled gunnery, proximity fuses to knock down fast moving aircraft, rockets, missiles, bazookas, grease guns, and jets. The Browning automatics, the Thompson machine guns, the Colt 45s stood our boys in good stead.

American industry cranked out 10 new fast battleships plus rebuilding and modernizing all the old ones, except Arizona and Oklahoma. In addition there were 24 new Essex class carriers, three giant Midway class carriers 1,000-foot long each, nine fast light carriers, 17 new heavy cruisers of the Baltimore and Oregon city class, 29 Cleveland-class 6-inch gun cruisers, a dozen Atlanta class anti-aircraft cruisers, 500 destroyers, 350 new submarines, and about 10,000 other ships.

Along with that, the Army got millions of trucks, 250,000 tanks, and about 200,000 highly advanced aircraft. Plus all the uniforms, boots, socks, belts, underwear, overcoats marching packs, tents, supporting infrastructure-like bases, and floating dry docks. There were beds, hospitals, portable heaters, stoves, and water tanks. Oh yeah, and don't forget, gas, food, and ammunition for everybody, including our allies all over the world.

And last but not least -- two atomic bombs.

World War II gave us heroes beyond count. First there were the big names like MacArthur, Nimitz, Halsey, Eisenhower, and Patton. And they said cool things like,"I will return, " "Attack... Repeat , attack," and "Thee object of war is not to die for your country but to make the other guy die for his."

It was the citizen soldiers that did the heavy lifting. In the battle of the Atlantic, it was the anti-submarine forces and the Merchant Marine sailors. In Africa it was the Rangers, the armor, the infantry, and the artillery. In France, it was the whole army, especially the airborne. Over Germany it was the Air Force. In the Pacific it was the fleet and the Marines.

There were lots of special outfits, like the Red Ball Express, the Navy Seabees, the Frogmen, the Carlson's Raiders, and very special outfits like the Tuskegee Airmen, the Japanese-American Regimental Combat Team, and the Navajo Code Talkers. The vast majority was just regular guys, called up to do their duty, and they did it.

Once America was fully mobilized the Axis powers had trouble just staying in the game and they quickly collapsed. Once ashore in Europe, Germany was quickly overwhelmed and overrun by the combined might of the Allied armies.

The Japanese were proud and stubborn and might have cost many millions of lives. At the end of the war the Japanese resorted to suicide missions to strike at us. The incredible staying power of the Japanese had been proven in one bloody campaign after another. The banzai charges, and the Kamikazes shocked even the most battle hardened Americans psychologically. The message sent by the suicide attacks was born and withstood, but not understood. The message was delivered to Japan and the rest of the world via the B-29s. Enola Gay and Boxcar spoke louder, and were completely understood by everybody.

So it ended well, but the evil did not go away. Before the war, we were a largely naïve and innocent nation. After the war, we found that we still had much more to learn about war. The nuclear genie was out of the bottle.

There were other great powers in the world. Many great socio-economic and political movements were afoot. The Iron Curtain descended over Europe. The former colonies of the great powers became new independent nations in many cases openly hostile and belligerent towards their former masters.

The European empires all fell. The sun gradually set on the British Empire. China was overrun by Communist revolution. Everywhere communist satellite states were armed as proxies to aid the Soviet Union's expansion into the vacuum created by the collapse of the old colonial order.

The founding of modern Israel set the Islamic world afire. It created social unrest and political imbalance that has challenged and troubled America to this very day. The communist insurgents are more than willing to shoot their way to power. The Marshall plan saved Western Europe and Japan.

The parade of wars continued. In 1950, the North Korean communist army crossed the 38th parallel in South Korea overwhelming the week Western military presence there. American industry was once again called upon to manufacture vast quantities of war material. The GIs were called back from the homestead again.

Gen. MacArthur said, "Give me the Marines." At that time, the Marines were led by hardened combat veterans of World War II. This proved to be bad news for the North Koreans at Inchon, and the red Chinese at the Chosin Reservoir. Once again, new places became part of the map.

The thing about Korea was that for the first time ever in our history, our forces were not allowed to finish the job. We gave the enemy a good licking but we weren't allowed to win. For America, war had finally become an extension of politics by other means. Evil was allowed to continue. We let them off the hook. The unhealed wounds fester in Korea to this day.

Where did we fail? Where did we go wrong? The fact is the American people were not willing to support escalation of the war into another global conflagration. Korea was the wrong war at the wrong time. American heroism saved South Korea and possibly Japan. It stabilized eastern Asia bringing prosperity and peace to millions of people around the Pacific Rim. But it did not change Russia and China. They chose Vietnam and Southeast Asia for their next big push.

When President Kennedy introduced American troops into South Vietnam, he Americanized what had originally begun as a Civil War of national independence. The North Vietnamese communists with backing from Red China and Russia intended to unite Vietnam under a single Communist regime. It looked like Korea again; it turned out far worse for America.

This time, it was the wrong war in the wrong place for the wrong reasons. We didn't really understand what we were getting into. Because of that, we failed. Unlike South Korea, South Vietnam was not saved. We did not lose it on the battlefield. They could not stand up to us in a straight up fight. It was a guerrilla war, booby-traps, civilian atrocities, stabs in the back, and American traitors.

For Americans there was a distant ring of familiarity to it. In Vietnam the jungle was Indian country. It was cowboys and Indians again, only this time with machine guns and bombs. Tomahawks came back into style; the troops took souvenirs in the form of scalps, ears, etc. The only good gook is a dead gook. In 1968, the boys were generally raising hell and having things pretty much their own way. But all was not well back in America. A new generation coming of age, a rock 'n roll generation. A generation raised by television.

There was a whole theme park of social revolution going on back home. There was the civil rights movement. There was the feminist movement. Birth Control pills had given women newfound freedom from the restrictions of their biology. Therefore, the sexual revolution had also begun. People were experimenting with drugs. People were engaging in widespread civil disobedience. Media pundits and radical social activists were stirring things up everywhere, in every way.

Generally speaking, life was good for most people back home. The economy was booming. We had twenty-five cents per gallon gasoline, twenty-five cent bread, twenty-five cent cigarettes, two dollar drive-ins, and fifteen cent hamburgers.

Everybody was driving long, low, wide 400+cubic inch V-8s. The girls were wearing very short miniskirts, and the music was the best of all time.

And television connected all.

Every night the muddy, bloody, noisy horror was played out in the average family living room. It was possible to watch people's sons and brothers and fathers and uncles and nephews screaming and bleeding in Technicolor.

The lousy management of the war and a terrible waste of treasure and human resources led to an ever-growing antiwar movement. Left- leaning communist sympathizers pervaded the American media and throughout a large part of the academic intelligentsia within America's vast college and university system.

This mixed well with the hard partying, easy living, "it's all about me" baby boom generation, who didn't want to be drafted. A college deferment, a burned draft card, or a hideout in Canada was the path of many rebellious youths. Guys who believed in old-fashioned patriotic values were viewed as squares or patsies.

The country was being torn apart by multiple socioeconomic and political factions. The troops felt betrayed. As if the people back home didn't have their back anymore.

It was a sad time for America.

For the first time in our history, the American fighting man lost faith in their leaders. Discipline relaxed. The troops got high. Officers got fragged (killed by their own troops).

The titles of popular music told the story. In the beginning, it was "The Ballad of the Green Berets," and turned into "I ain't no senator's son," and finally, "Run through the jungle and don't look back again." It was time to go home.

The end finally came when the Communists signed a phony peace treaty. We handed the war over to the corrupt and incompetent and unwilling South Vietnamese. Then we bailed.

During the entire withdrawal, we watched the Communists build up their forces for the final assault. But there was no going back. The blockheaded whiz kids in Washington, the left-wing intelligentsia, and the bleeding heart social engineers had done their work too well. Vietnam was indelibly perceived as an unholy war.

The GIs came home in disgrace to lick their wounds. The generals and admirals sat in the Pentagon and contemplated how to reform and renew and prepare for the next wave of trouble.

In 1974, the draft was abolished for the first time since 1941, and a new military paradigm based on a professional standing army was begun. Just like when the Roman army changed from a conscripted force of amateur citizen soldiers to the professional legions of Marius and Caesar, so the American military establishment changed its doctrine and chose to rely upon professionally paid volunteers.

In 1980, Ronald Reagan was elected president and undertook to rebuild American military power. American ingenuity and high-tech prowess now proceeded to create a force so efficient and so formidable that the Soviet Union literally broke itself trying to keep up.

The Gulf War was a good war. Desert Storm proved to the world that America was once again the world's only true superpower. This time we were prepared, and even though the old Soviet bloc crumbled, the forces of Islamic extremism, begun with the founding of Israel, had matured into a global terrorist movement designed to attack the West at every opportunity. The most hatred was directed towards America, ally and protector of Israel.

The nature of war has changed. Mastery of air-land battle has made America supreme in any conventional set-piece battle (the classic formal confrontation between armies). But the war on terror is different. It is called asymmetrical warfare. In short, it is the Indian Wars and the gangster wars and the Cold War with spies and computers and killer flying drones all rolled into one. Its effects have changed our society.

We used to have a relaxed, carefree society. 9/11 changed that. In order to protect our citizens and our way of life, we have turned our country into a virtual police state in the name of homeland security.

Flying has become very inconvenient and the airlines themselves totter on the edge of financial insolvency. The joys and perks of flying have all but disappeared.

The Army is stretched to the breaking point, fighting insurgencies in Iraq and now again in Afghanistan. But the Iranians are building a nuclear capability with the help of our old enemy, North Korea (which has already produced its own bombs with the assistance of our own left wing appeasers). They are protected by our so-called friends Russia and China. It seems that we have forgotten Eisenhower's warning concerning not becoming involved in land war in Asia.

Nevertheless our young men and women are still doing a great job.

In ancient Rome, the doors to the Temple of Janus always stood open in time of war. In America, the gates of the Temple have stood open since the moment our forefathers stepped ashore. In between wars the country experienced short periods, when we literally did beat our swords into plowshares. But mostly, the doors of Janus stood open and they're open now, even today to this very moment.

It's like this about Americans in war: Americans don't want to go to hell. We have seen hell. We have raised hell. Hell is hot. Hell is where we send the bad guys. We will always give them hell. As long as we know who they are. And perhaps, more importantly, as long as we know who we are.

THE ENEMY

They did it. It was them.

Who is them?

You know the ones who hurt us. The bad
guys. The enemy.

Since the very beginning, Americans have
had enemies. It started with the land
itself. Harsh, wild, untamed, vast
distances, many adversities, many
hardships to endure and overcome. It was
done. The land was eventually tamed,
beaten even regrettably exploited.

More difficult to overcome were the
dangers and threats of other people and
peoples. Hence the enemy. The enemy
comes in many guises. Many faces. Many

ways. But his purpose is always clear. The enemy means to hurt us, bring about our demise, cause us to fail, cause us to lose, defeat us, destroy us.

Over the centuries America has had many enemies both foreign and domestic. Often the threat has been easily and clearly identifiable. Yet just as often the threat has been misidentified. Many times in our history we persecuted and made war on the undeserving. And in the worst cases we have discovered the enemy to be none other than ourselves.

One way or the other it can be said that the objective of the enemy is to deny us personally the freedom and initiative to pursue success, create joy in our lives and pass it on to our progeny, even to the point of taking our lives. The basic recognition of this premise was essentially laid down for Americans right at the beginning by the Declaration of Independence. It didn't end there.

Who then is the enemy today, right now? Who or what is the greatest threat to our nation, our culture, our character, and our personal individual identities?

We live in very complex times. There is great stress being pressed down upon every individual personally, as well as with our collective cultural institutions. All you have to do is channel surf for a couple of hours on TV, it and it is pretty easy to see that we are a nation clearly suffering from future shock.

The social, political, cultural, familial, spiritual, and personal fabric of the nation is being wrenched, ripped apart, punctured, stretched, and bent all out of shape, so as to be barely recognizable in many cases. Who is to blame? What is to blame? Who are they? How do we deal with them? The easiest answer to that is that the devil knows the first three questions and only God knows the answer to the last one.

However, if we consider a few matters and pay attention, it is possible to delineate and recognize how the enemy operates as he works us over. Let's talk now about the enemy and see if you also have perceived some of these patterns of behavior in your own experience.

In our time, the enemy has achieved much. In fact, it could be said that the enemy has managed to make reality stand on its head. How is this so? you would inevitably ask.

They begin by using a skillfully crafted logic of perversity which never fails to suck in the rebellious or the guileless.

They initiate all their efforts by claiming the moral ascendancy. They are always moral, they are always righteous.

The enemy's most successful model is best described as the heroic circle of social political and economic revolution and it generally follows the classical Marxist paradigm. It relies heavily on artistic sophistry combined with humanistic empathy towards the common good and the condition of the poor and the oppressed. In short they make up lies. These story-lies are then set forth to impart their message and thereby gain following.

They start by creating a situation, most often fictitious but with possible parallels to real life which make it sympathetic to people's subliminal feelings or gut intuition. In this situation, they describe or create a story of events whereby a person or persons are abused, exploited, and otherwise oppressed (call them the inferiors). These underdogs are able to, with the aid of God (or a key ethnic minority genius), to overthrow, supplant, supersede, overcome, or destroy, and ultimately replace their abusers (the superiors), who are almost always rich, conspirital, criminal, prejudiced, greedy, immoral, racists (and who are usually white skinned). Hence the myth of the noble ethnic racial revolutionary hero is born.

This hero is able to break through all personal, social, political, or economic barriers and succeeds against all odds in overturning the hated status quo. This is the very heart of the enemies' very successful strategy that has been used to undermine and discolor the most successful human adventure and glorious achievement, which is our United States of America.

They do it with fantasy and fiction and song. They focus on and work their way through a series of human arenas, such as popular youth culture, the world of sports, law and crime, sex and interpersonal relationships, religious affiliations, and finally politics.

Once they have succeeded in establishing a sympathetic political power base they then use that power to attack, downgrade, invalidate, or eliminate all opposition be it individual or collective. In other words anybody that disagrees with them is in for bad weather.

They do it by painting their opposition as racists, evildoers, or hate-crime perpetrators. In the end, all of their high-handed moral superiority turns out to be mere camouflage. A slick dodge to facilitate their skim and scam on the unwary and in the end, trapping their intended victims.

Make no mistake. The enemy is out to politicize, indoctrinate, manipulate and control every aspect of people's lives and more importantly, their individual social behavior. The tools are readily available to pull it off and there are many disgruntled personalities out there, apt to their control.

Modern media facilitates their efforts. Powerful spider web like bureaucratic regulation parasites all economic activity -- so much that the state is now to be considered a prominent and permanent multilayered partner in every venture, no matter how vast or minute. Of course all the while this is going on there is also the ever present cacophonic rain of slanted films, songs, advertisements, speeches, and educational indoctrination.

And if you dare to disagree? If you rock the boat? If you stand up to these pop-culture social trends most of which were conceived and entrenched by them, then you should get ready because they are coming after YOU. They are coming after you in every way, on every day. They will get you. They will attack you socially, politically, economically, and personally. Just ask celebrities who have made mistakes, social and political faux pas which fly in the face of the enemy's carefully contrived concept of politically correct.

Any demonstration of openly frank disagreement with their self-righteous philosophy will invite hostile retribution on their part. Depending on the degree of your objection you will be ostracized. You will be discredited, mocked, humiliated, assaulted, destroyed, eliminated, wiped out, or barring that, you will at least be re-educated.

In the name of national security we find
ourselves well along in the process of
creating a virtual police state. Most
Americans resent official intrusion into
their personal lives. We mostly try to
ignore it. We tend to bury our heads in
the sand thinking that if we work hard
and take care of our own business things
will eventually work out right. That is
classic American optimism. But while we
have not been paying attention the enemy
has been very very busy and also very
very successful.

That is why we all now find ourselves
increasingly trapped in a growing
evolving Orwellian nightmare. The simple
fact is our government is stepping all over
us. Government has become the number
one business career destination of choice.
It has become grossly oversize, grossly
overpaid, grossly inefficient, grossly
corrupt, and intolerably arrogant. On top

of that it has become unionized, and therefore politicized, and also fragmented into many hostile factions.

In the name of justice and to keep everything fair, we have produced millions of lawyers and each year we continue to add thousands more. What do lawyers do? The answer is lawyers litigate. This result is lots and lots of laws, regulations, and red tape, which causes the need for hundreds of thousands of bureaucrats to push all that paper around.

Our business and financial institutions have also grown very large, very rich, very smug, very arrogant, very greedy, but marvelously perfectly politically correct. They may operate on Wall Street but they totally own Main Street and their big money says it's going to be their way or the highway. Play along or so long.

We are paying too much for too little. We consume too much. We produce too little. And we whine and complain a lot about everything. Too many people expect somebody else to solve their problems for them and too often that somebody turns out to be Big Brother.

One half of the population wants to tell the other half the population how to live and they have the nerve to expect those with whom they may disagree and attack, to foot the bill for the change. In the end it amounts to the enemy orchestrating something being taken from someone who earned it, and handing it to someone else who didn't, whereby the middleman who brokered the deal profits most from the exchange.

Now just who is who?

Maybe it's time we all looked in the mirror and did some soul-searching. We all know who is who and what's what and what's right and what's wrong. In part we may all be to blame but if you look behind the curtain and read between the lines and wiggle your nose and trace back who benefits most from the most perverse and cockamamie ideas, you can smell the POLECATS!

As stated at the beginning of this essay, we live in very complex times. The America of today is not the America of the past. We evolve it is inevitable. It is true that many of our greatest principles and character traits and stereotypes still endure; such is the magnitude of their universal virtue. Nevertheless we are being whittled away slowly and the strain is beginning to show.

The enemy is out there in many ways and many guises. Truly we face a multiplicity of threats but as stated in the beginning of the essay the identification of the threat is the key.

Consider for a moment the evolution of United States as a great civilization and compare it to say, ancient Rome as a baseline. At this particular time in our history the United States would have to be placed in a position corresponding to where the Romans were when the Republic was failing and the Imperial Principate was beginning.

This was a time when after a period of mighty conquests (in which the Romans greatest enemies were overcome) tremendous social and demographic change engulfed Roman culture and Roman society bringing on sudden rapid social and economic imbalances which ultimately overwhelmed the Republic's institutions and the people who administered them. Into this scenario entered great power, great wealth, pride, greed, institutional corruption, and moral decline.

The Romans were a strong people and their power and influence were to dominate the world for another 500 years. The influence of their culture persists even to our time today. Yet the fact is that Romans were ultimately done in by their enemies and in many cases, they were their own worst enemies.

Consider the United States in these terms. The government of the Roman Republic was designed to run a city, not an empire. The government of the United States was designed to run a federation of independent states, not the world.

The Romans ultimately fell because the members of their ruling hierarchy destroyed each other. The fact remains that the Roman Empire was built by men with a common clearly identifiable language, culture and understanding of how their government was supposed to work and did work. Everybody had a seat at the table. Everybody had a share in the success according to their stature and position within the society.

Things began to go wrong when great wealth and personal power and special privilege ran unchecked among the aristocracy. This was the beginning of the end. Like the classical Greeks before them. Like the other great Western powers that came after they were destroyed by factionalism, greed, and selfishness.

It is clearly evident that the United States of America is threatened by the same forces. There are a number of oligarchical conspiracies at work within our country involving our government as well as our business institutions and our various intelligentsia. Since the end of World War II, our government and our leaders have been more than willing to prostitute the virtues of our nation in order to gain World Empire and influence. Much to our dismay, it is beginning to be self-evident that the actions and decisions of our leaders in recent decades have been not only grossly incorrect, but potentially criminally negligent.

The government, the media, and much of academia today are rife with One World, one government, and multicultural philosophy. "We have to save the earth," is one excuse. "Oppressed workers of the world unite," is another. "It is our moral duty to lead others out of their darkness," is still another. Under this do-gooder guise we have managed to export our industrial base to places like China, India, and Brazil. We have also managed to abort some 40 million or so American babies and replace them with 100 million foreign nationals -- both legal and illegal -- who do not necessarily wish to assimilate our culture.

This is not good news for the broad mainstream of the American middle-class which is experiencing a steady consistent disenfranchisement, while at the same time our national sovereignty erodes and disappears. Is it possible that the demographic balance has been tipped radically on purpose? You decide. These are things that people don't like to talk about or think about. It's too complicated. It's too much to figure out. Let somebody else deal with it.

It is this kind of thinking which has brought us to where we are today. Treachery, apathy, and mendacity have infected us. The rot has set in. In the near future, we will seriously regret allowing our industrial base to shrivel and our infrastructure to decay. When the Chinese and Indians and maybe the Brazilians can out produce us, they will also be able to outspend us and maybe even begin to think that they can out fight us. Consider again the Roman baseline.

Even deep into the fourth century, Rome's greatest enemies -- the barbarian tribes in the north and the Persians in the East were unable to defeat or overwhelm any portion of the empire. However they were constantly launching raids and planning expeditions and inciting trouble along the borders always hoping to lure a Roman army into a trap to overwhelm it. A Roman catastrophe was always used by the enemy to demonstrate Roman weakness in the eyes of all those under Roman influence and control. Could a similar situation even today be evolving along the vast rim of Asia? You decide.

We are fortunate in one respect: Our prominent citizens have not yet begun to kill each other. Neither has our military establishment turned its loyalty away from the population in favor of radical loyalty to its popular leaders. However recent government statistics show that there are now twice as many people working in federal state and local government than there are people working in basic manufacturing. The statistics should be sending out alarm bells to concerned people in all walks of life.

It should be remembered that America's huge industrial base is what permitted us to win two World Wars. It also allowed us to establish the highest standard of living ever achieved on Earth for not only ourselves but the rest of the world. And it provided the cutting edge of all our technical innovations and advancements throughout our entire history.

Our industrial might is the true engine of wealth, prosperity, and opportunity and should not be allowed to pass into the hands of other nations who wish to supersede us and worse. You can't have less than half the population working to provide for people who think that it is their job to tell the providers not only what to do, but what they should think, and how they should behave. This is an anathema, and a sin. This is the true path to catastrophe and the ultimate fall of Western civilization.

So what do we do? We are surrounded by enemies at home and abroad, as well as within, and we don't even know who most of them are.

One answer might be a return to good old-fashioned American common sense. In the much admired world of American professional athletes, they always say when you get knocked off your game, you have to go back to fundamentals. Back at the beginning in 1776, the Declaration of Independence clearly stated that we pledged our lives, our fortunes, and our sacred honor upon our principles even unto death. Two hundred some odd years later, it still makes sense that if we don't stand together as one, we will go down one by one. Or as they said back in the day, "We must all hang together or we will surely hang separately." Or perhaps, put more colorfully in the American vernacular, "If the enemy wants us, let them come and get us but they better bring it."

The enemy within involves a completely different set of problems. Now we are talking about character. It was character that built this country as surely as it was character that built ancient Rome. It will require character to renew and strengthen the old principles and ethics of the founders, the settlers, the immigrants, the inventors, the scientists, the engineers, the artists, the writers, the leaders, and the geniuses. If we can renew ourselves and re-concentrate our talents and innovate and think big, the way the 19th and 20th century Americans did, we will be all right.

Treachery and treason are words that seem to have gone out of style in our time. Political correctness has weakened our sense of national unity, damaging both our political and philosophical consensus. Today, there exist powerful and wealthy conspirital factions, both within and outside the country, working under the guise of moral and humanitarian concern, all the while desiring secretly to divide, disrupt, and ultimately destroy our social cohesion, our political consensus, and ultimately our nation.

We must find a way to rid ourselves of these people who thrive within the highest levels of our government, business, and academic institutions, paying themselves millions of dollars as they plunder and pillage our wealth and transfer it in most unfair and criminal fashion. Only if we are able to identify and unmask these monstrous threats will we be able to continue to develop and enrich our American dream. As stated in the beginning of this essay, the correct identification of the threat is the key.

Having done that, who and what is there to fear? Answer: Having identified the threat properly and correctly, we need only"Fear God and dreadnought." Then and only then, will "this great nation endure as it has endured."

THE AMERICAN FUTURE: COMMENTS AND CONCLUSIONS.

WHAT DOES THE FUTURE HOLD?

If you study   the under-language closely you might say that "the future's so bright, we gotta wear shades." On the other hand, looking at all the hateful content and derision, looking at the increasing deviancy (the old-fashioned term is perversion), listening to all the new age double-speak, one could say the future holds dark portent.

As a people, we face myriad threats to the life we have known, and to the continuance of "THE DREAM." Many people still don't recognize threat; many do and are growing increasingly alarmed. We all sense the increasing rush of time, drawing us nearer to some great looming unknown. Events transpire as we all turn our personal treadmills faster and faster. The price of survival is going up. The world is again becoming a very dangerous place.

WHAT ARE WE TO DO? WHAT WILL WE DO?

We don't have much cause to have faith in our leaders. The record of our politicians over the last five decades is not encouraging. As the under-language reflects, politicians are perceived as prostitutes and crooks. They constantly "straddle" issues" or "sit on the fence," avoiding confrontation and controversy.

They tried to play both sides, always seeking out the lowest common denominator to provide some form of maximum voter support, which serves to take care of them personally. They play games with our lives and gamble with our country's future.

They have saddled us with incredible national debt. They have saddled us with a huge tax burden. They have constructed a vast money-sucking bureaucracy. They are now permitting government employees to form unions, thereby politicizing the government workforce and creating an über-class. They have turned government into a more lucrative career destination than the private sector or academia.

Government employees now make nearly twice the income of their counterparts in the private sector, along with elite benefits, and they can't be fired. Specially appointed "czars" and powerful bureaucrats hire yuppie lawyers to write new rules, regulations, and laws that Congress doesn't even bother to read, but still rubber-stamp its approval. They are responsible for all the new ways to control us and collect money. All this to pay for an ever-evolving, social-welfare police state.

Every aspect of everybody's life is being monitored, taxed, controlled, indoctrinated, and regulated with a complex array of forced sociopolitical obligations. It is as if our lives are no longer our own. People are becoming apathetic, cynical, and chronically misinformed. The nation is losing its sovereignty, surrendering its military superiority, and giving away its economic superiority, while at the same time supporting the gradual creation of a world government that will make slaves of us all.

Basically, they have scammed us -- put us together -- with the ultimate intention of disenfranchising us. They've taken trillions of dollars in military research, paid for by the American taxpayer, and given it away or allowed it to be stolen by foreign interests, whose long-term agenda is to supersede that of the United States.

Since World War II, they have consistently prostituted the virtues of our country in order to establish a super-rich world elite, allied to world collectivists, all bent on establishing a world government, controlled by the right people supporting their politically correct philosophies and agendas and their condescending new morality.

Almost none of it will benefit the American people and their long-term security and standard of living. The greatest transfer of wealth in history has been accomplished by judicial and bureaucratic fiat, right before our very eyes. And it is still going on now, as we speak. And if you look around at current events and the trouble we are in, it's pretty easy to see that the efforts are bearing fruit.

So there is the problem and the answer:

It is time to wake up, America, and signs are everywhere that this is becoming so. We have been grazing far too long. We have become rich, fat, spoiled, lazy, and soft, as well as smug, cowardly, sneaky, and corrupt. And it stinks to high heaven!

But a time is now at hand. "Our destiny draws nigh," as they say in Church. The time is coming when each of us is going to have to stand up, suck it up, ante up, and stick together, and start looking out for each other.

The apex of history is approaching us, folks. The old-time America that we grew up in is beginning to look more and more like an endangered species. It is disappearing right under our noses . What are we going to do about it?

One thing is certain. Those who keep their heads in the sand are liable to get their asses singed when the "shit hits the fan" and "all hell breaks loose." Is the 21st century going to be another American Century? Or is it going to be a Chinese century? Or worse -- a world government international conspiracy century.

A lot of this is our own fault. We haven't been paying attention. We have allowed ourselves to be distracted, misguided, and deliberately deceived -- partly by our leaders, but also very much by our appetites. Let's face it, over the last 50 years or so we have been sold "a bill of goods" and we've been gullible, naïve, provincial, easy-going, optimistic, "suckers." We bought in. Now there are too many rules, too much red tape, expensive labyrinthine legal obstructions, intrusive social, political, and hypocritical moral scrutiny smothering and stifling our natural American creativity. They have us all wrapped up tight and hidebound, like dogies at a rodeo.

We need to re-break our shackles. America needs to be America again. Americans don't ever want to be second best. It is not in us to lose, it is not in us to be restrained. We need to stop, or at least ignore the losers, who are looking to take down America. We need to turn the tables around on them.

We need to get hungry again. We need to get hard and tough again. We need to do big things, things that nobody else ever dared or hoped to accomplish. Get the government and the bloodsuckers out of the way and break loose like gangbusters. Let the American dream breathe again.

We need to "Change" the laws to make it easier for good ideas to be brought forward. Re-Industrialize! Perhaps we could create a new computerized national idea bank, whereby creative people with visions and solutions would be guaranteed both credit and compensation for their ideas if acted upon by business and industry, government, or academia -- all this in addition to the current patent and copyright laws.

Adopt a comprehensive national industrial policy with the intention of assuring that American products and American innovations are manufactured here and exported abroad rather than the current inverted system whereby American products are manufactured abroad and re-imported at home, much to the benefit of our worldwide competitors.

We should build a new fleet of bigger, more-advanced space shuttles. Go back to the moon and build a permanent base. Build ships to travel to Mars. Establish a permanent colony there.

Rebuild the Interstate highway system. Rebuild 100,000 bridges that need replacing. Criss-cross the continent with "mag lev" high-speed trains.

In 1936, the expiration of the London Naval Treaty allowed the United States to begin building heavy warships. Many closed down. Factories had to be reopened. This was, in fact, the engine of prosperity that really pulled our economy out of the Great Depression. Why couldn't we do that again?

The whole point is that America should be leading the pack socially, morally, economically, and technologically. All the time, in all the ways, and every day. This is not only possible, it is absolutely necessary. We can do it, after all… "We did before we can do it again."

And God help those politicians and pundits who dare to tell the American people that they are going to be second best and that the time of American power and American economic preeminence is past!

We need to put a stop to all of these "effete-snob, politically-correct, do-gooder, yuppie, pinko, whiz kid, egg head, condescending nerd, losers, who think to arrange one big happy world with them in control and sitting in judgment of us all.

Gut reaction? "I don't think so, forget
about it, no way, up theirs, they can stick
that moral social engineer loser
doubletalk where the sun does not shine."

No obfuscation, remember?

To all of you "smug, arrogant, overpaid,
under-talented, manipulative, hide-
behind-the-curtain, chicken-shit, control-
freak asshole, bossy self-righteous,
overbearing, smooth son-of-a-bitch,
mother-fuckers." We know what you are.
We know what you are trying to do. And
we know who you are:

We are not going to stand by and let you
wreck it all. We will not be restrained.
We will not be limited. We will not see
our country turned into a socialist police
state of slaves, bastards, and cowards.

"This is America, Mother-Fuckers! Have guns; will travel. Remember?" "Don't piss down my back and tell me it's raining." There, how's that for a rant? That is the power of the Under-Language in action.

Scott Fitzgerald once wrote that the sin of America was the sin of Mozart massacred. He was right then, and it appears that he still is. Over the years, we have squandered vast resources for various misguided reasons, many of which served only to strengthen and nurture our enemies. This did not have to be so then, and it doesn't have to be so now or in the future. Remember one thing: We still have men and women who can do anything. All we have to do is be ourselves (our old selves that is). Steady on Boys. Keep the faith.

Let us make a big production out of it, the way we always do. Everybody gets a seat at the table. Everybody is welcome aboard. Everybody can contribute. Everybody can find a place.

There was once a place where the individual was held in highest honor, a place where the land and the environment were sacred and inviolable --a land of strong families, a land of righteous religious principles and humane philosophies with principles, as laid down by the founding fathers in the Constitution. Without exploitation. Without obfuscation. Without hidden agendas. Our land. Semper Fi Mac.

THE MOTHER LODE

1. All the way
2. Break as in giving me a break
3. Boy
4. By the numbers
5. Be cool
6. Cop out
7. Cool
8. Hard-core, hard way, hard man
9. Help, help out, help yourself
10. Harp, don't Harp!
11. Ducks in a row
12. Hot, hot stuff, hothead, some like it hot
13. Mustang
14. What goes around comes around
15. Flip the switch
16. Change up

17. Up beat

18. Downbeat

19. Take care of business

20. Pedal to the metal

21. Blow your mind

22. Agree to disagree

23. The bottom line

24. Heavyweight

25. Heavy hitter

26. A slugger

27. I don't swing that way

28. Swingers

29. This music swings

30. Just say no

31. Tooling along

32. Tokin' on a number

33. Dig that

34. Bronkin' buck

35. Hot rod

36. Drag racer

37. Pickup truck

38. What a drag

39. Rednecks

40. Crackers

41. Moonshiners

42. Hide out from the

43. The cops

44. The man

45. G-man

46. Law man

47. Call the shot

48. Packing heat

49. Tits

50. Boobs

51. Jugs

52. Rack

53. Bazoons

54. Boom boom

55. Demolition derby

56. Roller derby

57. Kentucky derby

58. Scuttlebutt

59. Jar head

60. Jirene

61. Motor mouth

62. Deep throat

63. Singing cowboys

64. Lighten up

65. Hog leg

66. Speakeasy

67. Check out

68. Hoofer with great legs

69. Fed

70. Ta tas

71. Gams

72. Squared away

73. Gung ho

74. Rust pickers

75. Squids

76. Nigger

77. Woolly head

78. Eggplant

79. Mulligan

80. Sambo

81. Tootsun

82. Midnight

83. Mogambo

84. Moor

85. Jive

86. Don't talk jive

87. Hey man, cut the jive

88. Malarkey

89. Snake oil

90. Check that out

91. Scope it out

92. The thing is

93. Your thing

94. My thing

95. Our thing

96. His thing

97. Her thing

98. Their thing

99. Do your thing

100. Go along for the ride

101. Taken for a ride

102. Gonzo

103. Phony

104. Bitchin'

105. Get mellow

106. Goof

107. Goof off

108. Goofball

109. Play hooky

110. Laid back

111. Hang

112. Hang back

113. Hang out

114. Hit man

115. Button man

116. Bite me

117. Eat shit

118. Eat shit and die

119. Nuts

120. Sucker

121. Suck up

122. Chump

123. Strunz

124. Psych out

125. Deliver the goods

126. Take the hit

127. Zap

128. Ray gun

129. See ya around

130. Get off

131. Bust

132. Bust his balls

133. Bust his stones

134. Brake his balls

135. Off the chain

136. Off his rocker

137. Rock me baby

138. Rock steady

139. Steady on

140. Steady as she goes

141. Right on

142. Rippin'

143. Dissin'

144. Mark twain

145. Yankee

146. Rebel

147. Blue belly

148. In a bad place

149. Whiz kid

150. Take the shot

151. He had his shot

152. A shot at the big-time

153. A lollapalooza

154. Brake the bank

155. A wrench

156. A mech

157. A tuner

158. A gun slinger

159. A shooter

160. A hitter

161. Let them off the hook

162. Make my day

163. They are in cahoots

164. A slow hand

165. They are asking for it

166. Fat chance

167. Go for it

168. Make your move

169. Make a move

170. A world of shit

171. The 'burbs

172. From the burg

173. Never give a sucker an even break

174. Skim

175. Skinflint

176. Tight ass

177. He squeezes the nickel till the
buffalo shits

178. Cheap skate

179. Oh yeah

180. That's what I'm talking about

181. Now you're talking

182. No tiki no laundry

183. Talk is cheap; it won't buy
    good whisky

184. Hero

185. Sub

186. Dagwood sandwich

187. Big Mac

188. Whopper

189. Hotdog

190. Loafer

191. Rich bitch

192. In the clear

193. A cheater

194. A gigolo

195. Cornutu

196. Do you want to live forever?

197. On the Fritz

198. On the fence

199. Kick the bucket

200. I'm going in

201. You go down there general

202. Back in the day

203. Chill out

204. In-your-face

205. So long

206. Hásta la vista baby

207. What's up Doc?

208. Sup

209. Dude

210. Mama

211. Sick puppy

212. Defective unit

213. Get down on it

214. You can't touch this

215. Awesome

216. Cool it

217. Cool your duals

218. Cool customer

219. Keep your cool

220. When the game is on the line

221. The iceman

222. Check it out

223. Shut up

224. Goof up

225. Screw up

226. Get it up

227. Lawyer up

228. Kiss up

229. Suck up

230. Fuck up

231. The blues

232. All hot and bothered

233. Hot as hell

234. It's all good

235. Homeboy

236. Hey

237. That's really something

238. Go for broke

239. Jughead

240. Jugears

241. Hog leg

242. Heater

243. Peacemaker

244. Bowie knife

245. Pig sticker

246. Barlow knife

247. Switchblade

248. Sling blade

267. Deal with it

268. Tough guy

269. Badass

270. Sideways

271. Go deep

272. End around

273. Drop back to throw long

274. Pay dirt

275. Get a life

276. Stir the shit

277. Turn on

278. Tune in

279. Dropout

280. Lets hightail it out of here

281. Skedaddle

282. Make like a tree and leave

283. Pasadena

284. We are out of here

285. Count me out

286. Poker face

287. Game ace

288. In it for the money

289. Don't beat around the bush

290. He stepped in it

291. He fell into it

292. The moon

293. The finger

294. The bird

295. Over easy

296. ·Save your bacon

297. Up shit crick

298. All or nothing

299. Hit 'em where they ain't

300. Get there first with the most

301. Cracker

302. Heel

303. Jacktar

304. Redneck

305. Hardtack

306. The goddam Chicahominy river

307. Old Man River

308. Huckleberry

309. He is a natural

310. Grits

311. Call off the dogs

312. Old Ironsides

313. Unconditional surrender

314. Kicking ass

315. I'm just saying

316. Deal with it

317. Forget about it

318. Younz

319. Girls with tight pants show a camel toe

320. Squeal

321. Read-out

322. Rat out

323. Drop a dime

324. Lay across the barbed wire

325. Take one for the team

326. Fake it

327. Fake 'em out

328. Cross 'em up

329. Double-cross

330. Bohemian

331. Beatnik

332. Hippy

333. Yuppie

334. Get high

335. Kick back

336. Laid-back

337. Game face

338. Stick 'em up

339. A chopper is a machinegun

340. A chopper is a motorcycle

341. A chopper is a helicopter

342. Put on my selling shoes

343. Put on my sheepskin

344. Almighty buck

345. The doe

346. The doe re me

347. The jing

348. The jack

349. A fin

350. A dime

351. A yard

352. A nickel

353. A three dollar bill

354. Dead Presidents

355. Ben franklins

356. The cabbage

357. The dope

358. Good dope

359. Bad dope

360. Good shit

361. Nasty shit

362. Queer

363. Shit out of luck

364. Short end of the stick

365. You can't have everything

366. By a nose

367. Came in last

368. Shalom

369. You bet your life

370. Your ass is grass

371. Pure as the driven snow

372. Not a chance

373. Not a snowballs chance in hell

374. You're dead meat

375. You're toast

376. No way, José

377. Don't bug me

378. High wire act

379. Lose your ass

380. Getting creamed

381. Soften you up

382. Pulled it out ,pulled it off

383. If you want something right, do-it-
yourself

384. Money can't buy love

385. Strung out

386. Put up job

387. Touch base

388. Luck flies out the window

389. Your shittin' me

390. No shit

391. That will be the day he

392. Once-in-a-lifetime

393. Any port in a storm

394. Don't spin your wheels

395. Don't jerk us around

396. Leave you in the dust

397. Take the controls

398. Fart up a storm

399. Kelsey's nuts

400. Caught them flat-footed

401. More than one way to skin a cat

402. You don't say

403. Time is a wasting

404. We're burning daylight

405. Over the hill

406. Coming down the stretch

407. Cover your ass

408. Out of hand

409. Over the top

410. That's a stretch

411. Taken off the table

412. Don't leave money on the table

413. Disappear into the woodwork

414. Out of the woodwork

415. Don't bite off more than you can chew

416. Hell hath no fury like a woman scorned

417. The whole ball of wax

418. The whole shebang

419. Jump out of my skin

420. Scared to death

421. Bored to death

422. The devil is in the details

423. Give the devil his due

424. Fly in the ointment

425. Throw a monkey wrench into it

426. You don't know diddly squat

427. You don't know your ass from your elbow

428. You don't know your ass from a hole in the ground

429. Let it lie

430. The man lays it down

431. It's all laid out in front of us

432. Fly by the seat of your pants

433. Up your ass

434. Up yours, Bub

435. Greenhorn

436. Tenderfoot

437. Mahoint

438. Going postal

439. Tell me about it

440. Put it where the sun does not shine

441. The grass is always greener on the other side

442. Standing tall

443. Bozo

444. Bimbo

445. The straw that broke the camel's back

446. Knock yourself out

447. Go piss up a rope

448. Artsy fartsy

449. Count on it

450. Still going strong

451. When you're screwed, you're screwed

452. You screwed up

453. A stitch in time saves nine

454. An ounce of prevention is worth a
     pound of cure

455. A penny saved is a penny earned

456. Small gains make a heavy purse

457. Hardball

458. Don't ask

459. Shake a leg

460. Break a leg

461. Give it to you straight

462. Dead to rights

463. Dumb as dirt

464. Dumb as a post

465. Dumber than a bag of hammers

466. One hand washes the other

467. I'll scratch your back if you scratch mine

468. A match made in heaven

469. A match made in hell

470. Out with the old in with the new

471. Be there directly

472. Be there straightaway

473. Ram it down your throat

474. Made it just under the wire

475. Nail your ass to the wall

476. Cut the jibber jabber

477. Oh fiddle faddle

478. You can run but you can't hide

479. The $64 question

480. Made in the shade

481. Cool as a cucumber

482. Cool as the other side of the pillow

483. In like Flynn

484. In for a penny in for a pound

485. Easy come easy go

486. That will be the day

487. When hell freezes over

488. All in a day's work

489. Good as gold

490. Bust your balls

491. Bust your chops

492. Now that's a horse of a different color

493. In a New York second

494. Back in a heartbeat

495. Things are getting out of hand

496. It's an inside job

497. He's an easy mark

498. She has eyes like a hawk

499. Buckeye

500. Hawkeye

501. You can lead a horse to water.

502. Sly as a fox

503. Memory like an elephant

504. Quiet as a mouse

505. Happy as a pig in shit

506. Happy as a lark

507. Stubborn as a mule

508. Solid as a rock

509. Light as a feather

510. Fat is a pig

511. Thick as a brick

512. Slippery as a eel

513. Wet behind the ears

514. Close out the show

515. Curtain call

516. The last Roundup

517. Tip of the iceberg

518. Whoops a daisy

519. Hot diggety dog

520. Put the kibosh on that idea

521. Too many eggs in one basket

522. Flat out tired

523. Your're either a hit or a turkey

524. Hang tough

525. Hang tight

526. Gee-whiz

527. What's your beef

528. Scratch for a living

529. Take a break

530. That's the clincher

531. That's a game changer

532. Give it some zip

533. Break the bank

534. Step on a crack break your
     mother's back
535. Just a spit in the ocean

536. Bump it up a notch

537. Ratchet it up

538. Water seeks its own level

539. That will fetch you a penny

540. Keep your house in order

541. That hit the nail on the head

542. She's a goner

543. By the skin of your teeth

544. Here's two cents worth

545. A tiger by the tail

546. Screwed blued and tattooed

547. Shit, shower and shave

548. Two bits

549. Six bits

550. Once he gets going, he really cooks

551. You lost me

552. Let me get my head together

553. Have a good one

554. Right back at you

555. Bank on it

556. I bought it for a song

557. It's in the bag

558. Making whoopee

559. You can't have it both ways

560. She's a bitch in heat

561. She's on the rag

562. Speak with fork tongue

563. Piece of cake

564. Easy as pie

565. Take a hike

566. Get lost

567. Spiffy

568. Go fly a kite

569. He is waiting for a shot

570. What a creep

571. Gives me the creeps

572. The sky is the limit

573. Open-ended

574. She is something else

575. Turncoat

576. Give 'em the slip

577. Window of opportunity

578. Tit-for-tat

579. Cock of the walk

580. Don't lollygag

581. Nothing is for sure but death and taxes

582. Well I'll be a monkey's uncle

583. Grin and bear it

584. They are coming on like gangbusters

585. What a dipshit

586. Johnny-come-lately

587. It's raining cats and dogs

588. He's a jerk

589. He is a jag off

590. By the dozen

591. He is a breadwinner

592. He is a winner

593. Sow wild oats

594. Easy as shooting fish in a barrel

595. It was a turkey shoot

596. Wet your sights

597. In a pinch

598. Short and sweet

599. Got myself into a jam

600. Hassle

601. No-brainer

602. Bell ringer

603. He is a fireball

604. He is a dirt ball

605. Blockbuster

606. Out of this world

607. Flying saucer

608. You'll be late for the funeral

609. He would be late for his own funeral

610. She is snotty

611. You look like shit

612. POS equals peace if shit

613. Let's call a spade a spade

614. Lights out

615. What a cornball

616. I get where you're coming from

617. I get it

618. They just don't get it

619. I can get it for you wholesale

620. It fell off the back of the truck

621. When you steal you need a fence to dispose of the goods

622. Eat my shorts

623. Ass hole

624. Spooky

625. Guys who worked for the CIA are called spooks

626. What a babe

627. Shit on a shingle

628. Bully beef

629. Better safe than sorry

630. For sure dude

631. That's for sure, that's for damn sure

632. Silence is golden

633. You can't make a silk purse from a sow's ear

634. Cold as a witch's tit

635. She is a bitch on wheels

636. He was an ornery old cuss

637. The whole 9 yards

638. The whole enchilada

639. The road to perdition

640. The Road less traveled

641. Head in the sand

642. Top notch

643. Top gun

644. That's a likely story

645. A bundle of laughs

646. Bundle of joy

647. The joke is on me

648. Funny Farm

649. Mealy mouth

650. Hold your horses

651. Read 'em and weep

652. First get your ducks in a row

653. Sitting duck

654. If it walks like a duck

655. Put up your dukes

656. It's a lemon

657. That's a gas

658. Rat race

659. A kick in the stomach

660. Spit in her face

661. Big palooka

662. A man with a plan

663. Jargon

664. Drop the ball

665. Fumble the ball

666. Ghost of a chance

667. That's swell

668. Hey man cut that jive

669. All that jazz

670. What a maroon

671. You're barking up the wrong tree

672. At the ready

673. Long johns

674. Long tom

675. Better late than never

676. Out of sight

677. We have them by the short hairs

678. We have them by the balls

679. I'm in hot water

680. A gig

681. That thing gives me the heebie-jeebies

682. The man gypped us

683. Jew you down

684. Come to God

685. Come to grief

686. Going at it

687. Like nobody's business

688. Two heads are better than one

689. Cold shoulder

690. On thin ice

691. It will come back to bite you in the ass

692. Wisecrack

693. Wisenheimer

694. A wise ass

695. It's clear sailing from here

696. Slaphappy

697. He's back in his shell

698. He plays with himself

699. Sticks and stones may break my bones

700. You broke his back

701. On the other hand

702. I read you loud and clear

703. In the tube

704. Nitty-gritty

705. Keep a hand in

706. Keep your pole in the water

707. Irons in the fire

708. She always has her nose in the air

709. We had the goods on him

710. She did some chiseling

711. Going like hotcakes

712. Going like gangbusters

713. Losing your grip

714. Get a grip

715. If at first you don't succeed

716. Don't go off half cocked

717. Just a gigolo

718. He is just a big lug

719. Pipe down

720. Zip it

721. Shut your trap

722. Zip your lip

723. Mind your own beeswax

724. Gangsters get bumped off

725. Eat my dust

726. Dog eat dog

727. The movie bombed

728. She's the bomb

729. A bucket of bolts

730. Only he can finagle that deal

731. Tinhorn

732. Tin ear

733. Throw him under the bus

734. Monkey shine

735. Monkey business

736. Ride the gravy train

737. Line up at the trough

738. Put that in your pipe and smoke it

739. Monkey see monkey do

740. Copycat

741. Cut a deal

742. Miss the boat

743. If you're not careful you get your ass in a sling

744. Don't put your tit in the ringer

745. Bring it on

746. That's not going to happen

747. High- hatting

748. Dirt ball

749. Dirty rotten rat bastards

750. Quit you're cribbing

751. Quit your griping

752. Quit your grousing

753. Once in a blue moon

754. Cabin fever

755. Hotshot

756. Oh my God

757. My sandbox

758. My crib

759. Now there's a girl with hair on her chest

760. Yep write down to her dick

761. Rat somebody out

762. Your momma

763. Who's your daddy

764. Blow your stack

765. Putting on the Ritz

766. No roughhousing

767. I've got me a stool pigeon

768. Flat foot

769. On the lam

770. Going to a hootenanny

771. She is a schmoozer

772. Going south

773. He really lays it on thick

774. Snatch

775. Pigeon

776. Built like a brick shit house

777. Follow the yellow brick road

778. Let's party

779. Get your shit together

780. Filthy lucre

781. Cute

782. He looks like a toad

783. Don't act like a jackass

784. For crying out loud

785. For Christ's sake

786. Pulling a train

787. We've been had

788. Give it the green light

789. Still carrying water for him

790. Way back when

791. Make your bones

792. Pay your dues

793. Straight from the horse's mouth

794. Horses ass

795. Broken down old nag

796. Horse feathers

797. By golly

798. He gives me the creeps

799. Like a bull in a china shop

800. The shit keeps piling up

801. Chances are slim and none

802. Over-the-top

803. A leopard can't change his spots

804. You can't teach an old dog new tricks

805. Green eyed with jealousy

806. Out for the count

807. Big fat tub of lard or shit

808. Cupie lips, cupie face

809. Hands off

810. A fling

811. Lipstick on a pig

812. Girly boy

813. At the end of the day

814. Moving forward

815. Talking heads

816. Never let them see you sweat

817. Talk the talk

818. Walk the walk

819. Double or nothing

820. Double down

821. Sandbagging

822. She is a big hit

823. Frog in my throat

824. Last one in is a rotten ?

825. Always blowing his horn

826. Walking on my grave

827. Dancing on my grave

828. Beating my time

829. Taking my time

830. Sound as a dollar

831. Bang for the buck

832. The buck stops here

833. Let's level

834. Door bartering

835. No Money down

836. Zero down payment

837. Drives like a little old lady

838. Kick the tires

839. Drive-by

840. Drive through

841. Fly by

842. He sang like a canary

843. He spilled his guts

844. He tossed his cookies

845. Road kill

846. Cough it up

847. Straight as an arrow

848. Broomstick up

849. Spite fence

850. Slugger

851. The batter in the fourth position is set
    to bat cleanup

852. Fastball

853. Curve ball

854. Homerun

855. A single

856. The double

857. A triple

858. Inside the park home run

859. Slide

860. Lay down a bunt

861. Get away

862. Pitcher

863. Southpaw

864. You don't know doodly

865. Right from the get-go

866. Right off the bat

867. I got burned

868. Stash

869. You know

870. Shoot the Moon

871. Unreal

872. Sticking in my craw

873. We are on a roll

874. Bad boy

875. Nip/tuck

876. For two cents

877. Two cents worth

878. Blew him away

879. Blowout

880. Hoofer

881. Grunt

882. G. I.

883. He's got no couth

884. She's got no clue

885. We Are all clueless

886. She's got class

887. They are running a game on us

888. Headache

889. Pain in the neck

890. Pain in the ass

891. Flash in the pan

892. Stud

893. Give a hoot

894. Everything from soup to nuts

895. Animal crackers

896. Mojo

897. Juju

898. Sweet 'n Low

899. He's loaded

900. Thig-a-ma-jig

901. Happy-go-lucky

902. The last nail

903. Close the deal

904. A nonstarter

905. Flip the bird

906. Give me the lowdown

907. Here goes nothing

908. Freak out

909. Flip out

910. Flies like a brick

911. No shenanigans

912. Wha cha ma call it

913. Hunker down

914. Upsie daisy

915. Ass backwards

916. Topsy-turvy

917. Crashed

918. What's cooking

919. Stick in the mud

920. Your goose is cooked

921. I'm done

922. No way

923. Kilroy was here

924. Give me five

925. High five

926. Dealing from the bottom of the deck

927. Double-dealing

928. Two timer

929. Stuff it

930. Sour grapes

931. Panhandler

932. The lone ranger

933. Tonto

934. Clean his clock

935. Shack up

936. Get off his case

937. The dust off

938. She poison

939. A glad hander

940. A blowhard

941. Cheez it the cops

942. It's all downhill from here

943. Bust his balloon

944. She has a great rack

945. She curls my hair

946. It makes my hair hurt

947. An accident waiting to happen

948. What a wreck

949. A clean shock

950. Bam bam

951. Chance it

952. Out of sight

953. Stacked deck

954. Stacked blonde

955. Underwater

956. Heebie-jeebies

957. One for the road

958. You're all wet

959. Get a load of this

960. Going NASA

961. Scumbag

962. Baloney

963. Time to hang it up

964. Never cast pearls before swine

965. We've got them covered

966. I'm all over it

967. Get over it

968. Blackballed

969. He breaking my back

970. Not worth spit

971. Okey dokey

972. Cinch the deal

973. Clencher, as in a broomstick up his ass

974. Going to the dogs

975. In a pine box

976. Can't see the forest for the trees

977. Blindsided me

978. Can't Win for losing

979. You can't buy luck

980. Were driving on fumes

981. Freezing my ass off

982. My eyes are shut

983. We blew it

984. Blow me

985. Blow job

986. Happy camper

987. We have a problem

988. A lump of coal in your stocking

989. Upstream without a paddle

990. Up shit creek without a paddle

991. By the hair of his ass

992. By the skin of his ass

993. No skin off your nose

994. Snake eyes

995. For all the marbles

996. The Square deal

997. Two left feet

998. Camel toe

999. Tangle toes

1000. The sweet spot

1001. A fire in his belly

1002. A bun in the oven

1003. I've had a belly full

1004. Jelly belly

1005. It's a tough job but somebody has to do it

1006. Passing the buck

1007. Two time loser

1008. The silence was deafening

1009. Pissed off

1010. Don't knock it till you've tried it

1011. That's a cockamamie idea

1012. And then some

1013. Piss on his fire

1014. Tit for tat

1015. Shooting the shit

1016. Can't catch a break

1017. Buck naked

1018. Spin it

1019. Spin out

1020. Rip roaring drunk

1021. Shit faced

1022. They caught us with our pants down

1023. It shit its pants

1024. If you take this here entrenching tool and lay it upside Charlie's head, I guarantee you, it will ruin his whole day

1025. It's got us Stumped

1026. Take the rap

1027. It's on the house

1028. Off the cuff

1029. The jig is up

1030. Low rent

1031. Lowlife

1032. Here's looking at you kid

1033. If you're going to shoot, shoot;
       don't talk

1034. A fair shake

1035. No time to lose

1036. 40 winks

1037. As far as I can see

1038. We are getting rolled

1039. It's a scam

1040. They ate our lunch

1041. Haste makes waste

1042. Drop-dead beautiful

1043. Blind as a bat

1044. Get up and go

1045. Hit the nail on the head

1046. Mother fucker

1047. Holy cow

1048. Go ape

1049. Can you dig it

1050. Kiss off

1051. Fuck off

1052. My ass is on the line here

1053. Bummed out

1054. What a downer

1055. That's an upper

1056. Out in the boondocks

1057. Bum fuck Egypt

1058. Scum bucket

1059. He threw me a curve

1060. That's a Mulligan

1061. Teed off

1062. High balling

1063. Scapegoat

1064. Sweep the dirt under the carpet

1065. Smack down

1066. Kickback

1067. On the same page

1068. What a ruckus

1069. Upside down on the loan

1070. Screw up a wet dream

1071. Dead meat

1072. More than meets the eye

1073. Doo doo

1074. You can catch more flies with honey than with vinegar

1075. Double trouble

1076. Take you down a peg

1077. The proof is in the pudding

1078. We were bamboozled

1079. Did it with smoke and mirrors

1080. Hoity-toity

1081. La-di-dah

1082. Is off his rocker

1083.   Three ends against the middle

1084.   Hangout

1085.   Hang in there

1086.   I can't hang

1087.   You'll get the chair for this

1088.   Happy days are here again

1089.   Go bananas

1090.   You're as fuzzy as a compass

1091.   He dropped his monocle

1092.   End of the trail

1093.   Round them up

1094.   A grifter

1095.   I get the picture

1096.   Don't do other people's laundry

1097.   Nebshit

1098.   He's waffling

1099.   Am I chopped liver?

1100.   I'm bushed

1101. I'm pooped

1102. I'm really beat

1103. Whodunit

1104. Turn on a dime

1105. My time your dime

1106. Your dime my time

1107. Brother can you spare a dime

1108. Five fingers on every glove

1109. Go jump in the lake

1110. Take a flying fuck at a rolling doughnut

1111. Just got the world by the balls

1112. He's got the world by the tail

1113. Really make it pay

1114. Put on the squeeze

1115. You're not going to weasel out on this one

1116. Playboy

1117. A player

1118. Money talks bullshit walks

1119. He stepped in shit

1120. He fell into the shit

1121. A world of shit

1122. A bug up your ass

1123. A bugaboo

1124. Bootlegger

1125. Rum runner

1126. Moonshiner

1127. Dirt bag

1128. Douche bag

1129. Scram

1130. Beat it

1131. Go away kid you bother me

1132. Hit the road

1133. No sweat

1134. Dude

1135. Stooge

1136. Big shot

1137. What a racket

1138. Feet first

1139. Jump in with both feet

1140. Get it off your chest

1141. Southern hospitality

1142. Old-fashioned recipe

1143. The retro look

1144. A bullet with your name on it

1145. Hook line and sinker

1146. Oh, dry up!

1147. He's got nerve

1148. It takes nerve

1149. He hasn't got the nerve

1150. You haven't got the nerve

1151. His nerves are shot

1152. Squatters

1153. Horse face

1154. Look me in the eye and tell me that

1155. A checkerboard

1156. A snake oil salesman

1157. A con man

1158. I've got news for you pal

1159. Reckon

1160. It is what it is

1161. Drop dead

1162. Just blowing smoke

1163. Shipshape

1164. Whistle clean

1165. Off the top of my head

1166. Learn your lesson

1167. Three bricks shy of a load

1168. I smell something fishy

1169. Something stinks in Denmark

1170. Don't count your chickens before

they hatch

1171. Looks like your chickens came home to roost

1172. They had us suckered

1173. They had us snookered

1174. Would you stake your life on it?

1175. Bar bag

1176. Pop star

1177. Popsicle

1178. Creamsicle

1179. Don't be an Indian giver

1180. He has a Teflon personality

1181. Carry his water

1182. You can't carry his jock

1183. You can't shine my shoes

1184. That's the whole kit and caboodle

1185. A pound of flesh

1186. She was a klutz

1187. Top banana

1188. Get fleeced

1189. Come up short

1190. Making book

1191. Preaching to the choir

1192. He's no altar boy

1193. Stand your ground

1194. We'll cross that bridge when we come
to it

1195. Across the River and into the trees

1196. Got them on the ropes

1197. Working on a shoestring

1198. Go Dutch

1199. Like fishing through an ice hole

1200. A done deal

1201. Burnout

1202. Outhouse

1203. He knows which side his bread is

buttered on

1204. Wing it

1205. The great unwashed

1206. Tops in taps

1207. We got stugatz

1208. Zilch

1209. The Shoe is on the other foot

1210. Now

1211. If the shoe fits wear it

1212. Jacked up

1213. Go straight

1214. A straight edge

1215. Mack the knife

1216. A straight guy

1217. A confidence man

1218. A confident guy

1219. Shit-kicker

1220. Yokel

1221. Hillbilly

1222. A hemp fandango

1223. Kansas City necktie

1224. Sissy

1225. Panty waist

1226. Cake eater

1227. Clicker

1228. Swinger

1229. A hail Mary

1230. A wolf in sheep's clothing

1231. Pin your ears back

1232. Waffle bird

1233. Pins and needles

1234. Pinhead

1235. Caboose

1236. No rest for the weary

1237. Only the good die young

1238. 3 pounds of crap in a 1 pound bag

1239. Jump on the bandwagon

1240. A walk in the park

1241. A Day at the Beach

1242. That is no day at the beach

1243. Tiptoe through the tulips

1244. Phony as a three dollar bill

1245. He is a dead duck

1246. Stick it to them

1247. Stick it

1248. Buffoon

1249. Draw a line in the sand

1250. Fast gun

1251. Gunslinger

1252. Quick draw

1253. Fast draw

1254. Draw the line

1255. Tycoon

1256. Stinks on ice

1257. Come again

1258. Fall on your face

1259. You let me down

1260. Hit the deck

1261. Settle his hash

1262. Frazzled

1263. Spill the beans

1264. You really cleaned his plow

1265. Ridge runner

1266. Get after you

1267. Get after them

1268. Hey Daddy-o

1269. A thing or two

1270. Down the toilet

1271. Down the drain

1272. On the ropes

1273. Beggars can't be choosers

1274. Lucky dog

1275. Suck hind tit

1276. Motley crew

1277. Cat got your tongue

1278. Too late we already drank the Kool-Aid

1279. Cockeyed optimist

1280. Far to go

1281. Say it ain't so

1282. What goes around comes

1283. around

1284. Blow the whistle

1285. The naked truth

1286. Use it or lose it

1287. In a pigs eye

1288. When pigs can fly

1289. Had to bite my tongue

1290. Bite your tongue

1291. Hold on

1292. Hold out

1293. Finders keepers losers weepers

1294. Get some

1295. Now we can really make some moolah

1296. Shit for brains

1297. Deadhead

1298. Brain-dead

1299. Don't be a schmuck

1300. It's a tossup

1301. I got dibs

1302. The last laugh

1303. He shot his bolt

1304. Shot his wad

1305. It burns me up

1306. Written in the cement

1307. Don't let it throw you

1308. Feeling the love

1309. Got a feel for it

1310. He really fell into at this time

1311. Weed can give you the munchies

1312. I don't give a rats ass

1313. What a twerp

1314. Wingnut

1315. Carrier out feet first

1316. Bottom feeder

1317. A hot hand

1318. Fast hands

1319. Sorry but my hands are tied

1320. Let bygones be bygones

1321. No bed of roses

1322. I never promised you a rose garden

1323. You're killing me

1324. Spare the rod and spoil the child

1325. Take you out to the woodshed

1326. Get off my back

1327. I don't want to step on anybody's toes

1328. That's all she wrote

1329. A woody

1330. She cries crocodile tears

1331. I get the hang of it

1332. Payola

1333. Lowball

1334. Swanky

1335. Make nice

1336. Quick on the uptake

1337. Slow on the uptake

1338. Download

1339. Upload

1340. Give me a vector; I'm coming home

1341. Take it up the middle

1342. A sure thing

1343. Your barking up the wrong tree

1344. Too hot to handle

1345. Can't figure him out

1346. Can't make it out

1347. Whatever

1348. By hook or crook

1349. Fucks like a mink

1350. Fuck like rabbits

1351. Now we can turn it over to the bean counters

1352. Now we smell blood

1353. Fat city

1354. You and what army

1355. Heavy lifting

1356. Up the kazoo

1357. Having a bad hair day

1358. She has big hair

1359. A backhanded slap in the kisser

1360. Get my drift

1361. Does a bear shit in the woods

1362. Pony up

1363. Hat in hand

1364. Now that is a site for sore eyes

1365. A shell game

1366. He is a con man

1367. It's a lulu

1368. They don't have a pot to piss in

1369. It's about time

1370. Timeout

1371. Times up

1372. The works

1373. Wiseguy

1374. Wise ass

1375. You can dish it out, but you

1376. can't take it

1377. It takes a lickin' and keeps on tickin'

1378. Have you taken leave of your

senses?

1379. Always get the money up front

1380. Its what's up front that counts

1381. Horseplay

1382. The boys are just horsing around

1383. Who's going to be the patsy?

1384. Heels to Jesus

1385. Percy in the playpen

1386. Wallpaper the closet

1387. Crib

1388. He is a hayseed

1389. Backwoods manners

1390. He's got a way about him

1391. The truth hurts

1392. Uh huh

1393. Loan shark

1394. Shylock

1395. Dear John

1396. When Johnny comes marching home again

1397. He beat me straight up

1398. Don't splash the pot

1399. Texas hold 'em

1400. Lucky strike

1401. I get your drift

1402. You don't throw your weight around

1403. Down home

1404. Down on the farm

1405. Down on me

1406. Wildcatter

1407. Suck it up

1408. When things are going against you

1409. Win one for the Gipper

1410. Cut he a check

1411. Limp as a wet noodle

1412. She's knocked up

1413. Six ways to Sunday

1414. A checkered past

1415. Don't let the grass grow under your feet

1416. Bull's-eye

1417. Bullshit

1418. Snug as a bug in a rug

1419. The argument has legs

1420. Blowing smoke

1421. Your argument doesn't water

1422. A fall from grace

1423. Knock it off

1424. Shoot your mouth off

1425. Make hay while the sun shines

1426. Katie bar the door

1427. Swamped

1428. Slammed

1429. Get real

1430. Play dumb

1431. They were layin' for us

1432. A dog and pony show

1433. He is a heel

1434. He is a shitheel

1435. Somebody has got a boo-boo

1436. Doesn't miss a trick

1437. You really came through for us

1438. Johnny come lately

1439. Putting on airs

1440. He has the right stuff

1441. The kind of man who won't back down

1442. My bad

1443. Effete snob

1444. Can you feel it slip away

1445. Slipping away from us

1446. Merry-go-round

1447. Grab the brass ring

1448. Big spender

1449. Look for his tell

1450. You're going to have to scramble

1451. Carry the torch

1452. Broken arrow

1453. Nuke 'em

1454. Don't skirt the issue

1455. Thinks his shit doesn't stink

1456. The bum's rush

1457. Doesn't have a pot to piss in

1458. He just wants to get into your knickers

1459. He just wants to get into your pants

1460. I never knew it could be like this

1461. Ooh la la

1462. Doughboys

1463. Boys in the hood,

1464. Homeboys

1465. Cadu

1466. Long, low, and wide

1467. Don't give a damn

1468. Well ain't that too damn bad

1469. Put a sock in it

1470. There's a sucker born every minute

1471. Do you think I was born yesterday

1472. We had a dry spell

1473. We hit a dry well

1474. Cash on the barrel head

1475. Looney tune

1476. Nobody likes hand-me-downs

1477. Nimrod

1478. Easy pickings

1479. Waiting for the other shoe to drop

1480. How in God's green earth

1481. It's beyond the pale

1482. They threw him under the bus

1483. Tied to the road tracks

1484. Here is your num, num

1485. Smack dab in the middle

1486. A little dab will do you

1487. We were snookered

1488. They fell flat on their face

1489. Knock him on his ass

1490. Roll up your sleeves

1491. You bet your bottom dollar

1492. That is a crock

1493. If you don't like it lump it

1494. He was a loose cannon

1495. She had a screw loose

1496. Not playing with a full deck

1497. I expect to be paid in cold cash

1498. Dick weed

1499. Ass wipe

1500. Fucktard

1501. Are you talking to me

1502. Are you kidding me

1503. Look me in the eye

1504. Look me in the eye and say that

1505. Say it to my face

1506. Okay shoot

1507. Soldier on

1508. Flea circus

1509. Raising hell

1510. Our ship came in

1511. Business before pleasure

1512. Ante up

1513. It seems to have a mind of its own

1514. Hit the skids

1515. A towheaded child

1516. He's yellow

1517. Clam up

1518. That's a slippery slope

1519. Dark days are upon us

1520. It's in the can

1521. Your worst nightmare

1522. The only thing that exceeds your

1523. stupidity is your ignorance

1524. Cream always rises to the top

1525. Run silent run deep

1526. 18 wheeler

1527. Breaker breaker

1528. Call sign

1529. Huddle up

1530. Get on your case

1531. The truth and nothing but the truth

1532. So help me God

1533. Riverboat act

1534. Jump through the hoop

1535. A straight face

1536. Striptease

1537. Cock tease

1538. Get along little doggie

1539. Who do they

1540. Hoop snake

1541. Assume makes an ass of you and me

1542. Beg steal or borrow

1543. Don't tread on me

1544. E pluribus Unum

1545. Gone with the wind

1546. Duh

1547. A bad egg

1548. Polecat

1549. Playing possum

1550. No, none nicht nada

1551. Just leave things well enough alone

1552. Redskins

1553. Injuns

1554. Tomahawk

1555. War paint

1556. Wampum belt

1557. Benedict Arnold

1558. Francis Marion the Swamp Fox

1559. Yankee doodle dandy

1560. Uncle Sam

1561. Bury the hatchet

1562. A hard case

1563. Hobo

1564. The boss

1565. Corn bread

1566. Hominy grits

1567. Collard greens

1568. Southern fried chicken

1569. Pasta fasul

1570. They don't know whether to smile, spit, or swallow

1571. Why do you have to make such a big

production of everything?

1572. Hells yeah

1573. Hell yes

1574. Hell no

1575. Oh hell

1576. What we have here is failure to communicate

1577. He's asking for it

1578. Lucille

1579. Maybelline

1580. Cadillac

1581. Get it

1582. Don't call it in

1583. Go looking for trouble and you will find it every time

1584. 44 magnum

1585. Magnum V8

1586. Rocket V8

1587. Get whacked

1588. Whack off

1589. Beat you like a redheaded stepchild

1590. The franchise

1591. Special ops

1592. Get your mind right

1593. Fuckin' aye

1594. Taking care of business

1595. Air superiority

1596. Death from above

1597. Take the high ground

1598. To enable

1599. Giddy up

1600. That put a hitch in his giddy up

1601. Hitch your wagon to a star

1602. A man's got to do what a man's got to do

1603. They are going to get it up the ass with a backhoe

1604. Far out

1605. Way rad

1606. Gnarly

1607. Out of the picture

1608. What's wrong with this picture

1609. Pass the hat

1610. Your razzin' me

1611. Flabbergasted

1612. Cover your ass

1613. I've got your back

1614. I'll be back

1615. Fiddlesticks

1616. Bunko

1617. The bomb squad

1618. Swat team

1619. Delta team

1620. Airborne rangers

1621. Force recon

1622. Special forces

1623. Navy seals

1624. Going to hell in a hand basket

1625. I dig it

1626. We were swept away

1627. Sour grapes

1628. Commie

1629. Pinko

1630. Enough to choke a horse

1631. Gag me with a spoon

1632. Dungarees

1633. Blue jeans

1634. Civvies

1635. Khakis

1636. We don't have to show you no stinking badges

1637. On Saturday night they're going to have a hootenanny

1638. Fleadick

1639. Leatherneck

1640. Air land battle

1641. Vertical monopoly

1642. Horizontal monopoly

1643. Playing monopoly

1644. There's no business like show business

1645. Give them the old one two three

1646. There is no substitute for cubic inches

1647. Tin lizzy

1648. There is a wolf in sheep's clothing

1649. Nothing but net

1650. Jumpshot

1651. Clobbered

1652. Wipeout

1653. Mountain man

1654. 49er

1655. Carpetbagger

1656. Scalawag

1657. Hooker

1658. Skank

1659. HIV

1660. Five and 10

1661. Sugar tits

1662. There is no law west of the
Pecos

1663. Wanted dead or alive

1664. Thicker than fleas on a dogs

1665. back

1666. Rug munchers

1667. Screwed her brains out

1668. Fucked her brains out

1669. Gay

1670. Homo

1671. Ride the white horse

1672. Toot

1673. Nose candy

1674. Quaalude

1675. Sopor

1676. Black beauties

1677. Meth

1678. Peyote

1679. LSD

1680. Psychedelic

1681. A bad trip

1682. Trip out

1683. Road hog

1684. Hells angels

1685. Bumping uglies

1686. Throw it in there

1687. Hijack

1688. Pick your marbles

1689. Lose your marbles

1690. Riff raff

1691. I'm hip

1692. Hitting on her

1693. Bling

1694. Raise a stink

1695. Skin flint

1696. Good to go

1697. Up the ying-yang

1698. In one fell swoop

1699. Wild horses couldn't keep me away

1700. Shake and bake

1701. Living on the fault line okay

1702. Hoodwinked

1703. Trick up the car

1704. I've got eyes on it

1705. Not worth a continental

1706. Stick around

1707. Did you buy a rice burner

1708. Truer words were never spoken

1709. Make no bones about it

1710. No doubt about it

1711. Count me in

1712. You can count on me

1713. Cutting-edge

1714. Stretch the envelope to the limit

1715. Outside the box

1716. Outside the envelope

1717. Jiminy cricket

1718. Gosh, golly gee

1719. Mad as hornets

1720. A hunch

1721. A standup guy

1722. Give them an inch, they take a
mile

1723. Beachcomber

1724. Beach bum

1725. Jinxed

1726. Don't put a jinx on us

1727. Here's a black cat

1728. Were underwater

1729. Your ass in the sling *

1730. What a horse's ass

1731. Mindfuck

1732. Get on my nerves

1733. That one is wrapped too tight

1734. Sleep tight don't let the bed bugs bite

1735. He got my goat

1736. Break a leg

1737. Not up to snuff

1738. Throw the bum out

1739. Take a powder

1740. Rubberstamp

1741. Doesn't amount to a hill of beans

1742. He's over the hill

1743. Going under the knife

1744. Shit happens

1745. Got your head up your ass

1746. Get over the hump

1747. Gold plated

1748. Solid gold

1749. G-string

1750. T-back

1751. Spandex

1752. Numb nuts

1753. Turn over a new leaf

1754. Get rich quick scheme

1755. Pie in the sky

1756. Throw them out on their ear

1757. Cook the books

1758. Head-to-head

1759. An old mossback

1760. Be a good sport

1761. The magic bullet

1762. The rising tide lifts all boats clear

1763. Shake things up

1764. Don't quibble over it

1765. You're nitpicking me

1766. You're splitting hairs

1767. He's up to something

1768. Kite a check

1769. The turnaround finally came

1770. They're giving us the runaround

1771. Seize the moment

1772. Yeah baby

1773. Let's get down to brass tacks

1774. A snarky remark

1775. Hurry up and wait

1776. Duke it out

1777. Stick to your guns

1778. If it's worth doing is worth doing right

1779. Namby-pamby

1780. Drop dead gorgeous

1781. Down in the dumps

1782. Down home

1783. Jazz man

1784. Play that git fiddle

1785. He drives a thunder chicken(T-bird)

1786. Isn't that sweet

1787. How sweet it is

1788. Hold on tight

1789. White knuckle it

1790. Chopping wood

1791. They hold all the cards

1792. What's good for General Motors is good for the USA

1793. See the USA in a Chevrolet

1794. Ford found on the road dead

1795. Ford fixed or repair daily

1796. Beam me up, Scotty

1797. Don't fuck around

1798. Hang up

1799. She hung up on him

1800. Time of your life

1801. A good kid

1802. Party girl

1803. A party

1804. Happy trails to you

1805. Back in the saddle again

1806. Thugs

1807. Scarf it up

1808. Kickoff

1809. He is just showboating

1810. A riverboat act

1811. One fell swoop

1812. A fast shuffle

1813. A smooth operator

1814. Wet your whistle

1815. Aces and eights

1816. Doesn't have a leg to stand on

1817. He still wet behind the ears

1818. Mark my words

1819. Come up smelling like a rose

1820. I wash my hands of it

1821. Going ga ga

1822. A grand

1823. He's worth his salt

1824. My ears are burning

1825. 100 large

1826. Git 'er done

1827. Cracker jack

1828. Head games

1829. They had us buffaloed

1830. Think global act local

1831. Freaks and geeks

1832. Can you get us off the hook

1833. A big goon

1834. Life of Reilly

1835. We've got our foot in the door

1836. In a nutshell

1837. And that's that

1838. Heads or tails

1839. Winner take all

1840. Sucker punch

1841. Writing is on the wall

1842. We've got it made in the shade

1843. Sink or swim

1844. Fat chance

1845. Arm twisting

1846. Talking turkey

1847. We've got to hand it to you

1848. Green in the gills

1849. Palaver

1850. Chump change

1851. Blabbermouth

1852. Every day and twice on Sundays

1853. Eat crow

1854. It all boils down to this

1855. Time to hit the hay

1856. He palmed it

1857. I'm down with it

1858. Burning the candle at both ends

1859. Turning a buck

1860. Take the fall

1861. You are going down

1862. Don't cotton to strangers

1863. Other fish to fry

1864. It all comes out in the wash

1865. True blue

1866. Everything but the kitchen sink

1867. Throw in the towel

1868. As the crow flies

1869. Got something up his sleeve

1870. I'm holding all the aces

1871. She's back on her high horse

1872. Get down to the nitty-gritty

1873. Bully pulpit

1874. Going at it with a hammer and tong

1875. Butter or guns

1876. Mick

1877. Kraut

1878. Pollack

1879. Dago

1880. Guiney

1881. Greaseball

1882. Wop

1883. Hammerhead

1884. Above and beyond

1885. Just around the corner

1886. Over the rainbow

1887. The twilight zone

1888. One way or another

1889. Our backs to the wall

1890. He bought the farm

1891. A guy is going to need

1892. Bolt the check

1893. Crack upside the head

1894. Play stinky finger

1895. Take me to your leader

1896. Good vibrations

1897. Good vibes

1898. Barbecue

1899. Creole

1900. Taken for granted

1901. No cherry picking

1902. Look behind the curtain

1903. Don't rock the boat

1904. Pick your poison

1905. Gunnery sgt

1906.   Mortal coil

1907.   Hey, bob

1908.   Hey bud

1909.   Hey buddy

1910.   Hey Mac

1911.   Hey pal

1912.   Put out

1913.   Step up your game

1914.   Step up to the plate

1915.   Step up

1916.   Pull a heist

1917.   Schtupped

1918.   Rub his nose in it

1919.   Everything is hunky Dory

1920.   Sharpshooter

1921.   Logrolling

1922.   The People's choice

1923.   Dark horse

1924. Favorite son

1925. The squeaky wheel gets the grease

1926. I spoke my piece

1927. Old-school

1928. Have you got shit in your ears

1929. It's not rocket science

1930. You will be one

1931. I owe you one

1932. Zipper head

1933. Slope head

1934. Raggin'

1935. The check is in the mail

1936. Here's mud in your eye

1937. You're playing with dynamite

1938. Icky

1939. I bet you dollars to doughnuts

1940. Don't hold your breath

1941. Deaf as a post

1942. Dunderhead

1943. Slapdash

1944. The old saw

1945. On the run

1946. It's right in front of your nose

1947. His bark is worse than his bite

1948. Hit the ground running

1949. You make your bed you lay in it

1950. A rabbits foot

1951. Native son

1952. Ass over tea cups

1953. The right stuff

1954. Organization man

1955. No problem

1956. Not a problem

1957. By trial and error

1958. Take a load off

1959. You bet your bippy

1960. We don't have a prayer

1961. Old glory

1962. Rebel yell

1963. Dog soldiers

1964. He really knows his shit

1965. Crabs

1966. Nips

1967. Wait up

1968. Get back on your feet

1969. Standup

1970. The dog ate my homework

1971. I'll take the fifth

1972. Never saw him before in my life

1973. Hollywood and Vine

1974. Run to daylight

1975. In God we trust

1976. Who cut the crusts off your PB&J

1977. Pillow talk

1978. Happy hour

1979. Toss your cookies

1980. Load the dice

1981. Make book

1982. Badabing, badaboop, badabop

1983. Zigzag

1984. A dogleg

1985. You ain't nothing

1986. Chicken out

1987. He is chicken

1988. Chicken shit

1989. Shot in the back

1990. Play the player

1991. Hook 'em and book 'em

1992. You send me

1993. High maintenance

1994. Woolgathering

1995. He is yellow

1996. A yellow stripe runs down his back

1997. Turned his lights out

1998. The white lady

1999. The brown lady

2000. Mary jane

2001. Mother lode

2002. A tough cookie

2003. Working both sides of the street

2004. Nick name

2005. Getting your bearings

2006. In that neck of the woods

2007. Caterwauling

2008. Bare-bones

2009. Sick at heart

2010. Eat your heart out

2011. One for the money

2012. With their tails between their legs

2013. Leave them alone and they'll come

home

2014. Get over yourself

2015. Thumbs-up

2016. Nothing happens till somebody saw something

2017. The big Kaduna

2018. Smokey the bear

2019. I don't have cooties

2020. Stunad

2021. Off the deep end

2022. Have your cake and eat it too

2023. The Sweet smell of success

2024. No free lunch

2025. What a sap

2026. A pet peeve

2027. Snap out of it

2028. White man speak with forked tongue

2029. Pudgy

2030. Jungle bunny

2031. It's a dud

2032. Step over the line

2033. He crossed the line

2034. They crossed the line when

2035. When push comes to shove

2036. Wake and bake

2037. That put a smile on his face

2038. Do you mind?

2039. Mind your P

2040. Mind over matter

2041. One-of-a-kind

2042. Second story man

2043. He's got fast hands

2044. A pig in a poke

2045. When God made him he broke the mold

2046. Superstar

2047. Right as rain

2048. Put a smile on his face

2049. Scared shitless

2050. Out of whack

2051. To get whacked

2052. Off the record

2053. On the QT

2054. We go way back

2055. Rock them sock them

2056. How about

2057. Give me a reason

2058. Honky

2059. White trash

2060. High yellow

2061. Octoroon

2062. The business end

2063. The boys want their cut

2064. To cut in

2065. Not cutting it

2066. That doesn't cut it

2067. Sent up to the big house

2068. Moved up to the front burner

2069. Put it on the back burner

2070. For the time being

2071. In the groove

2072. Groovy

2073. Time to pull up your socks

2074. Stake your life on it

2075. Are you willing to bet your life on it

2076. My lucky day

2077. Hit the bricks

2078. Cruising for a bruising

2079. Off the rails

2080. Taken with a grain of salt

2081. You've got your hands full

2082. She has a handful

2083. Easy as 123

2084. He is a load

2085. We got the shaft

2086. Stand down

2087. Mook

2088. Jamoke

2089. Anything you say

2090. Poppycock

2091. I am really steamed

2092. Laying down on the job

2093. Make a fuss

2094. Kick up a fuss

2095. Start a ruckus

2096. A humdinger

2097. Watch it, Pilgrim

2098. Milling around

2099. Head in the clouds

2100. Get your head out of the clouds

2101. Harebrained

2102. What's up Doc?

2103. They have got it in for you

2104. Rubbed out

2105. In the Dickens

2106. Last call for alcohol

2107. Goodnight Irene

2108. Going steady

2109. Pinned down

2110. You are your own worst enemy

2111. I skeeve

2112. Jet set

2113. Crazy as a bed bug

2114. A gentleman's agreement

2115. Every trick in the book

2116. A set up

2117. Hunkered down

2118. Lend a hand

2119. Throw them a rope

2120. I 'm a soul man

2121. Ditto

2122. Go Fuck yourself

2123. Not a chance in hell

2124. Don't knock it

2125. Till you've tried it

2126. Sic 'em boy

2127. Sic 'em Buck, Lassie, White Fang,

2128. Rin Tin Tin

2129. Low hanging fruit

2130. Peckerheads

2131. Suit yourself

2132. Catch as catch can

2133. Wetback

2134. Beaner

2135. Spaghetti bender

2136. Snake in the grass

2137. Son of a bitch

2138. Peel off

2139. Pimps and Ho's

2140. I fell for her act

2141. She's buying my act

2142. Get them to buy in

2143. They bought in

2144. Attaboy

2145. Way to take out the trash

2146. We got kicked out

2147. Time to kick back

2148. He wants a kickback

2149. Local yokel

2150. We don't kowtow

2151. Trim

2152. Things could get really hairy

2153. It's hairy in their

2154. One of the great mysteries

2155. Smartass

2156. He's off on a lark

2157. Just a passing parade

2158. You got everything coming to you

2159. Space head

2160. Dumbbell

2161. What a wiener

2162. He's a whiner

2163. Stow it

2164. Shoot yourself in the foot

2165. I swear on my mother's grave

2166. Hard cash

2167. Hard money

2168. Hand money

2169. I love the smell of napalm in the morning

2170. Rat fink

2171. Snort a line

2172.   Doing lines

2173.   Line dancing

2174.   Go bonkers

2175.   Having a blast

2176.   A blast from the past

2177.   Hard up

2178.   Angel dust

2179.   To barge in

2180.   A sitting duck

2181.   I'm afraid it's going to make a great
        deal of difference to a great many
2182.   gentlemen"

2183.   Bad ass

2184.   Sniff it out

2185.   Corny

2186.   Old Casey

2187.   You can't take it with you

2188.   Start from scratch

2189. He's no spring chicken

2190. Let's hustle

2191. The seven-year itch

2192. Horny

2193. Dew on the lily

2194. Everything is coming up roses

2195. Brick head

2196. Love canal

2197. You scared the pants off me

2198. We scared the pants off them

2199. What a crock of shit

2200. Losing your nerve

2201. I got the nerve

2202. Pretty gnarly

2203. That's the ticket

2204. Put it to bed

2205. Sand scratcher

2206. Strong-arm

2207. Own up to it

2208. Walk the line

2209. Hit the booze

2210. I got the blues

2211. Turn out the lights the party's over

2212. He's on the beam

2213. In the loony bin

2214. A huckster

2215. This places a dive

2216. She's a diver

2217. A hick from the sticks

2218. Highfalutin

2219. Put on airs

2220. Call the shots

2221. Rough waters

2222. Hogwash

2223. A stovepipe

2224. The heat is on

2225. The heat is off

2226. Hurly-burly

2227. The burning question

2228. Not worth a lick

2229. Hand over fist

2230. What's your angle

2231. Running around like a chicken with its head cut off

2232. You got a problem?

2233. Are you talking to me?

2234. Don't mince words

2235. If he makes a move plug him

2236. Bust a cap in yo' ass

2237. A lackey

2238. All night long

2239. A sammich

2240. A sangwich

2241. You better man up

2242. They're having a powwow

2243. No tomfoolery

2244. Clean as a whistle

2245. You've got me on pins and needles

2246. First string

2247. Second string

2248. Third string

2249. Fourth straight

2250. You're stringing me along

2251. Get squared up

2252. Spooked

2253. Stroker

2254. Jacktologist

2255. Spill your guts

2256. Drawdown

2257. Buyers are liars

2258. Pipe smoker

2259. Go hog wild

2260. No tattletales

2261. Old granddad

2262. Johnny walker

2263. Southern comfort

2264. Jim beam

2265. Flustered

2266. That is a cock and bull story

2267. Stop riding him

2268. You're running him down

2269. You can be sure if it's Westinghouse

2270. Seniors

2271. Money-back guarantee

2272. Oldsmobile rocket V-8

2273. It's a Hemi

2274. Hump day (Wednesday)

2275. It always rains on Monday morning

2276. Don't mean to rain on your parade

2277. Singing in the rain

2278. Touchdown

2279. Looking to get your neck stretched

2280. A dime a dozen

2281. It's just a gag

2282. Let's head for the barn

2283. Straight-laced

2284. We hit a gusher

2285. Wildcatters

2286. A bad rap

2287. My mouth dropped open

2288. Fruit of the loom

2289. DVDs

2290. BVD's

2291. Knock your block off

2292. Skivvies

2293. Nuke 'em

2294. Have a go at it

2295. Really going at it

2296. Terminate with great prejudice

2297. Fallout

2298. Roadmaster

2299. Peterbilt

2300. Kenworth

2301. Western star

2302. Diamond Reo

2303. Bulldog

2304. Six by

2305. He couldn't hit a bull in the butt with a bass fiddle

2306. Whatever floats your boat

2307. Get your rocks off

2308. Outside the lines

2309. It's a beautiful thing

2310. He's a powder puff

2311. A little discombobulated

2312. Hang down your head

2313. Drain the weasel

2314. Go through them like crap through a goose

2315. Get your mind out of the gutter

2316. Tried to ditch them

2317. Glitz

2318. Showbiz

2319. What a pickle Puss

2320. There's a couple of swell guys

2321. Star of the silver screen

2322. He could not hit water if he fell out of a boat

2323. Get your name up in lights

2324. Make you a star

2325. Think outside the box

2326. Whim worshipers

2327. He got racked up

2328. Rack them up

2329. On the mend

2330. Let's face it

2331. Good moves

2332. We were suckered

2333. Smarter than the average bear

2334. Put our heads together

2335. Let it all hang out

2336. Kill them all

2337. You kill me

2338. Install a kill switch

2339. Overkill

2340. Killing around

2341. If looks could kill

2342. Hey three on a match

2343. Tough mugs clam up

2344. They wouldn't sing

2345. We might have to lean on these guys

2346. They don't see things our way

2347. Ebonics

2348. Put that on your hat

2349. Keep it under your hat

2350. Get cracking

2351. He's got a stiff back

2352. Stretch the envelope

2353. Supped-up

2354. A stock car

2355. Golden boy

2356. The real deal

2357. Get your kicks

2358. He really rode the rough off her

2359. Take your lumps

2360. Rough necks

2361. Mouthing off

2362. Something got into you

2363. Logjam

2364. Top-of-the-line

2365. Running your mouth

2366. SSDD same shit different day

2367. Home on the Range

2368. There's no place like

2369. Jukebox

2370. Jukejoint

2371. Juke 'em out

2372. Schuckin' and jivin'

2373. Buckaroo

2374. We are heading for the last round up

2375. Ready for a screen test

2376. Can't quite put my finger on it

2377. You got a heavy heart

2378. That's a lot of hogwash

2379. Let's get baked

2380. She's a kook

2381. She's kooky

2382. Get bumped off

2383. First to feel the pinch

2384. A fly in the ointment

2385. Pours a church mouse

2386. Let's get it on

2387. What's eating you?

2388. The first to feel the pinch

2389. Out here there is only the quick
and the dead

2390. Poor as a church mouse

2391. Don't mess around

2392. Don't mess up

2393. Don't mess with it

2394. This isn't working

2395. Don't be so crabby

2396. Beaucoup bucks

2397. It doesn't do anything for me

2398. What if you done for me lately

2399. Just business

2400. Sit it out

2401. Stick it out

2402. Be prepared to sit this one out

2403. Gitty up

2404. That will put a hitch in your gitty up

2405. Amped up

2406. We can see through that

2407. Red dog

2408. On her back

2409. Wise up

2410. Something to put us over the top

2411. Snatch and grab it

2412. School of hard knocks

2413. Hot lips

2414. Who's your daddy?

2415. Come to Papa

2416. Damn Yankees

2417. Let's shake on it

2418. Winner, winner chicken dinner

2419. Your average Joe

2420. A clutch hitter

2421. Go to guy

2422. Clutch hitter

2423. A knuckle sandwich

2424. On the level

2425. He is legit

2426. Your ass is itchy

2427. Tough titty

2428. The wrong side of the tracks

2429. So this is how the other half lives

2430. The good life

2431. He's got a gimmick

2432. Would you hit that?

2433. I think he is tapping that ass

2434. Don't candy coat it

2435. I get around

2436. You ain't seen nothing yet

2437. Breaking in to the business

2438. Crash the party

2439. Okay that's a wrap

2440. It's a birthday

2441. A dirt nap

2442. By the farm

2443. I'll see you in my dreams

2444. Now you've gone and batted the beehive

2445. Now you've done it

2446. Do the job

2447. On-the-job

2448. A quarterback controversy

2449. Got cold feet

2450. A foot up your ass

2451. They are showing their teeth

2452. We are fed up

2453. Not going to take it anymore

2454. Keep the faith

2455. Never sell out

2456. Never rat on your friends

2457. Keep your mouth shut

2458. Don't give up the ship

2459. Big knobs

2460. Love handles

2461. Strut your stuff

2462. Mooch

2463. A grafter

2464. A panhandler

2465. On the grift

2466. A hobo

2467. On the make

2468. Fucknuts

2469. Boost a car

2470. The fix is in

2471. She dances the cooch

2472. What a rube

2473. Brainstorming

2474. Brain fart

2475. Brainwash

2476. Heavens to Betsy

2477. Heavens to Murgetroid

2478. Off to the races

2479. Beat 'em around the face
and head with a telephone book

2480. Blackjack

2481. Call your bluff

2482. Get off the hook

2483. My asses dragging

2484. Like a spent whoopee cushion

2485. You lie like a rug

2486. Not all it's cracked up to be

2487. Giving me grief

2488. Ali Ali oxen free

2489. Open a can of worms

2490. Open a can of whup ass

2491. He's a rat Fink

2492. We're in for a shakeup

2493. Make it past

2494. Hicks from the sticks

2495. Going through the roof

2496. It's a longshot

2497. Old fuddy-duddy

2498. Old fogey

2499. Perception is reality

2500. What's your deal?

2501. Have a go around

2502. He's a flunky

2503. He's a putz

2504. Schmuck

2505. A milk box

2506. Make a run at it

2507. We had a ball

2508. Keep your eye on the ball

2509. She likes to ball

2510. Will they play ball

2511. The kid has balls

2512. Meanest bitch that ever balled
       for beads

2513. You done for me lately

2514. Pussyfooting around

2515. Get to the point

2516. Upstairs girl

2517. When you do something wrong you
       get cracked for it

2518. Jimmy crack corn

2519. Got in a crackup

2520. They all got smashed

2521. Mama's boy

2522. Booby-trap

2523. She is a lush

2524. Across the road

2525. From a Main line family

2526. A mainlander

2527. Give them the treatment

2528. The old soft soap

2529. Just razzin' 'em

2530. I'm sorry mom

2531. A pile up

2532. Piling on

2533. Pull fast one

2534. Rainmaker

2535. Keepsake

2536. Ask me nice

2537. Make it rain

2538. Played you for a sucker

2539. Buddy up to him

2540. You know something

2541. You got more sand than most

2542. This horse has a lot of bottom

2543. Another day another dollar

2544. Damage control

2545. Time to open the wallet

2546. Who cut the cheese

2547. Schooch over

2548. Whoops shanked it

2549. Drogue shoot

2550. Just like cookie cutters

2551. The real magilla

2552. You want I should

2553. Clodhoppers

2554. Sod busters

2555. Make a run for it

2556. Lock stock and barrel

2557. It's not over till the fat lady sings

2558. Land in the hoosegow

2559. Not going to happen

2560. The big easy

2561. Cotton picking

2562. Pick you apart

2563. Get the first down

2564. Over my dead body

2565. Here we go again

2566. Back to square one

2567. Runs like a top

2568. Old betsy

2569. I don't think so

2570. Don't touch my junk

2571. Till the fat lady sing

2572. The fat lady sang

2573. It's a wrap

2574. Piggybank

2575. Not a deal breaker

2576. Take them out to the woodshed

2577. You scratch my back and I'll

scratch yours

2578. Throw a monkey wrench

2579. For the love of Mike

2580. For the love of Pete

2581. For Pete's sake

2582. Stonewall them

2583. Shucks

2584. The roscoe

2585. He tried to weasel out

2586. Riffraff

2587. A wart healer

2588. Gum up the works

2589. Take the bull by the horns

2590. No dog in

2591. We're splitting hairs

2592. Shove it down their throat

2593. On the arm

2594. It's bogus

2595. Start the ball rolling

2596. Crazy in love

2597. Ace in the hole

2598. Just a bunch of cowboys

2599. To get ambushed

2600. A roll in the hay

2601. I smell blood in the water

2602. Don't cut corners

2603. He rolled over

2604. I'd like to wring his neck

2605. Cut a check

2606. Float a loan

2607. Up the wazoo

2608. Get to the root of it

2609. Knuckleheads

2610. Now we are in a pickle

2611. Save his own skin

2612. By the skin of his nose

2613. Jamboree

2614. Half a tank

2615. Half in the tank

2616. My dogs are sore

2617. You look like death warmed over

2618. Work it out for yourself

2619. Until the cows come home

2620. Get a handle on it

2621. All bets are off

2622. A longshot

2623. Play it as it lays

2624. Take what the defense gives you

2625. Scarf it down

2626. Is this a great country or what

2627. Read them and weep

2628. He lucked out

2629. A bum steer

2630. Quit ragging on him

2631. Typhoid Mary

2632. Take the bitter with the sweet

2633. My Way or the Highway

2634. E-book

2635. Guns or butter

2636. Money upfront

2637. When it finally shakes out

2638. A drop in the bucket

2639. Ants in the pants

2640. Come back to bite you in the ass

2641. Schmaltz

2642. Dicey

2643. Pennies from Heaven

2644. Run out of rope

2645. A cup of Java

2646. The short end of the stick

2647. Get it up

2648. Run out of steam

2649. Phooey

2650. Here's the hair of the dog that

2651. bit me

2652. Keep an eye out

2653. Knock me over with a feather

2654. Smart aleck

2655. Keep your powder dry

2656. All hell is breaking loose

2657. He's a drip

2658. Roll with the punches

2659. Babes in the woods

2660. A jalopy

2661. Get the gist

2662. Jump her bones

2663. Let the cat out of the bag

2664. Up to snuff

2665. Time to skedaddle

2666. A song and dance

2667. No turning back

2668. Give me some skin

2669. Right on the money

2670. A white knuckle ride

2671. Going like a bat out of hell

2672. Knock on wood

2673. A lot of tripe

2674. Then his ear

2675. Twist his arm

2676. Stuck in my craw

2677. Play you for a sucker

2678. Hullabaloo

2679. I'll be a monkey's uncle

2680. No dice

2681. A Burr under my saddle

2682. Pay through the nose

2683. Talk turkey

2684. How do you like them apples

2685. Nice threads

2686. Let it eat

2687. The hay is in the barn

2688. Porn scanners

2689. Feel her up

2690. Cop a feel

2691. Raunchy

2692. Come up with something

2693. Lily liver

2694. Put a stake together

2695. I'll stake you

2696. She's a freak

2697. Freaky

2698. Buck the system

2699. Kick sand in my face

2700. To get knocked off

2701. I'll call you back

2702. Toodles

2703. You're going to be the death of me

2704. Enough with the wisecracks

2705. A natty dresser

2706. Take that job and shove it

2707. You can kiss my ass

2708. A one hopper

2709. Right Field

2710. Leftfield line

2711. Ground ball

2712. Shortstop

2713. Sky pilot

2714. Get some strange

2715. Blondie

2716. Golly

2717. Gosh

2718. Oh my gosh

2719. Grody

2720. In the pink

2721. Bug the system

2722. Cornpone

2723. Thank your lucky stars

2724. Who is running the show

2725. I got your number

2726. I'm good

2727. Turn out the lights

2728. Blitz them

2729. Sack the quarterback

2730. One game at a town

2731. No dog in him

2732. A heart of gold

2733. Knock 'em dead

2734. Buckle up your chin straps

2735. He muffed it

2736. Muff diver

2737. Bushwhacker

2738. Drop your cocks and grab your socks

2739. Stick it in and break it off

2740. Reach down and suck it up

2741. Don't be a pest

2742. Zone blitz

2743. Time flies

2744. Ain't that a kick in the ass

2745. Take out the trash

2746. A day on the farm

2747. The town pump

2748. Are you tapping that

2749. Wouldn't hit it

2750. Phony baloney

2751. Open up a can

2752. Of whup ass

2753. As in whup yo' ass

2754. Gutless wonders

2755. 90 Day wonder

2756. Mighty quiet out there, too quiet

2757. "¿Quién sabes?"

2758. Plug 'em

2759. Give him two slugs in the belly

2760. or in the head

2761. He caught a slug

2762. "Yubba, dubba, do"

2763. He can dish out, but he can't

2764. take it

2765. I can take it

2766. That is a suck up

2767. Arc light

2768. Kill them all and let God sort them out

2769. With a few Marines and enough ammunition we can

2770. kill them all

2771. Collateral damage

2772. A daisy cutter

2773. He put us together

2774. Get your head wrapped around
it

2775. Good and plenty

2776. Who's on first

2777. We own it

2778. Do you savvy

2779. That's what we do

2780. Old leather

2781. Stick together

2782. A brown study

2783. He dotes on her

2784. Gas guzzler

2785. Contraption

2786. Gimme some elbow room

2787. It not advisable to meddle in other
people's business